A

THE NEW BEST OF FINE WOODWORKING

Working with
Routers

Working with
Routers

The Editors of
Fine Woodworking

The Taunton Press

The Taunton Press
Inspiration for hands-on living®

The Taunton Press, Inc., 63 South Main Street, PO Box 5506, Newtown, CT 06470-5506
e-mail: tp@taunton.com

Distributed by Publishers Group West

Jacket/Cover design: Susan Fazekas
Interior design: Susan Fazekas
Layout: Susan Lampe-Wilson
Front Cover Photographer: Jim Dugan
Back Cover Photographers: (top left) Tom Begnal, courtesy *Fine Woodworking,* © The Taunton Press, Inc.; (top right) © Dennis Preston, courtesy *Fine Woodworking,* © The Taunton Press, Inc.; (bottom right) Mark Schofield, courtesy *Fine Woodworking,* © The Taunton Press, Inc.

The New Best of Fine Woodworking® is a trademark of The Taunton Press, Inc., registered in the U.S. Patent and Trademark Office.

Library of Congress Cataloging-in-Publication Data

Working with routers / Editors of Fine Woodworking.
    p. cm. -- (The New best of fine woodworking)
  ISBN 1-56158-685-4
  1. Routers (Tools) 2. Woodwork. I. Fine woodworking. II. Series.
TT203.5.W67 2004
684'.08--dc22

                              2003020533

Printed in the United States of America
10 9 8 7 6 5 4 3 2 1

The following manufacturers/names appearing in *Working with Routers* are trademarks: Accuride®, Amana Tool®, Biesemeyer®, Black & Decker®, Bosch®, Carb-Tech®, CMT®, Davenport®, DeWALT®, Eagle America®, ENCO®, Foredom®, Freud®, F S Tool℠, Grizzly®, Hartville Tool®, Hitachi via Mechanics®, Rout-R-Lift™, Jet®, Jet Equipment & Tools®, Jorgensen™, Leigh®, Lexan®, Loctite®, Makita®, Masonite®, Melanine®, Milwaukee®, MSC Industrial Supply Co.℠, Multi-Router®, NH Northern℠, Plexiglas®, Porter-Cable®, Speedmatic®, Reid Tool Supply Company®, Sears℠, Skil®, Starrett®, SY®, Teflon®, The Wooodworker's Store℠, Trend-lines℠, Tru-Grip®, Clamp-N-Tool Guide®, Watco®, WD-40®, Woodtek®, Woodworker's Supply℠, Xacta®

Working wood is inherently dangerous. Using hand or power tools improperly or ignoring safety practices can lead to permanent injury or even death. Don't try to perform operations you learn about here (or elsewhere) unless you're certain they are safe for you. If something about an operation doesn't feel right, don't do it. Look for another way. We want you to enjoy the craft, so please keep safety foremost in your mind whenever you're in the shop.

Acknowledgments

Special thanks to the authors, editors, art directors, copy editors, and other staff members of *Fine Woodworking* who contributed to the development of the articles in this book.

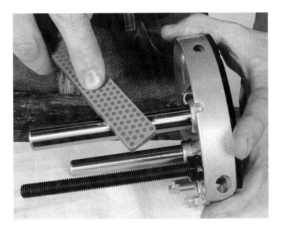

Contents

Introduction

When you take into account its cost and size, the portable router wins hands down as the most resourceful power tool in the woodworking shop. With this machine you can shape profiles; make duplicate copies; cut grooves, rabbets, dovetails, and mortise and tenon joints. For most woodworkers, the router is an essential power tool just because it can do so much, whether you are working with solid wood, sheet goods, or veneer.

I started out woodworking with only a few hand and power tools. No tool did as much for me as a fixed-base, 1-hp router.

One of my first large projects was a bookcase, and I put that router to good use. The router allowed me to cut the joinery—rabbets and dadoes—and then joint the edges of the raw plywood (using a straightedge as a guide), and finally trim the solid wood edging flush to the plywood surface. Considering the router cost me only $50, it accomplished more than its fair share of work.

In the 20 years since, I've collected a few more routers as well as several accessories and jigs. The most valuable accessory is my shop-built router table, which in many small shops, has taken the place of

the spindle shaper. A router table allows you to cut miles of moldings, machine fine joints, and do all of these tasks with precision and ease.

Dovetail jigs are another useful accessory for the router. Although I still like the look of hand-cut dovetails, when I need to crank out a batch of drawers and time is limited, I rely on my dovetail jig. And like most router accessories, you can choose to buy one or to make your own.

As woodworkers have come to rely heavily on this tool, manufacturers have kept pace with the demand for better routers in all types and sizes. There are plunge routers, fixed-base routers, routers appropriate for handheld work, and routers so big they're best installed in a table. Routers can be had with variable speed (to safely run large-diameter bits) and better mechanisms for precise adjustments. No one router will excel at all tasks; if you get serious about woodworking, you will eventually own more than one.

The router stands out as one of the most innovative twentieth century inventions for the woodshop. As you'll see from the chapters in this book, which have been excerpted from the pages of *Fine Woodworking* magazine, woodworkers continue to invent new jigs and methods for

getting the most out of this tool. Although the router is considered one of the safer tools in the shop, like any power tool, you need to understand its workings and safe operating procedures, which are also covered here. Armed with that knowledge, the router's potential is limited only by your creativity.

—Anatole Burkin, editor of *Fine Woodworking*

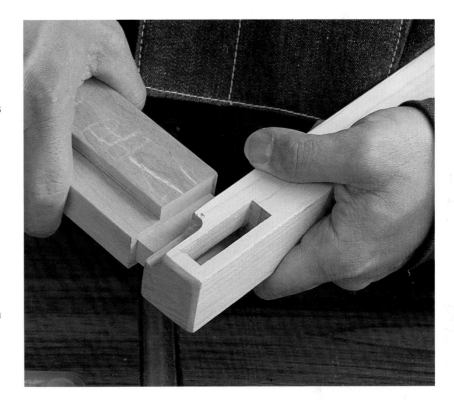

Routing Safe and Sound

BY PAT WARNER

When you lose control of a router, whether totally or just a little, it's the workpiece that most often gets messed up. Now and again, you'll chip or break a bit. And if you're really unlucky, you will get hurt. Keep this in mind: Most router bits rotate at a speed in excess of 20,000 rpm. When something goes wrong— a grab, a dig, a jolt to the machine, bad things happen fast. I have had my fingernails trimmed mighty close by a dovetail bit before I knew what happened.

Router safety is essentially a matter of controlling the router and securing the workpiece (and vice versa on the router table). Safety considerations are therefore intimately related to the quality of the cut. The safest routing technique will by and large yield the best finished surface.

Here are some tips to help you produce the quickest, smoothest, and safest cuts with a router.

1. Some Bits Bite Back

Not all router bits are created equal. Some are far less capable of handling the stresses of cutting wood and will break easily. Some are prone to other problems, such as burning or catching in the cut. Recognizing bits that need particular care will help you keep them from biting you and your work.

TRAPPED! Cutting a sliding dovetail buries the bit in the work. If the router can't be pulled up and away, the bit is trapped and needs careful guidance.

Long, Thin Bits Are Fragile Thin bits with cutting-edge lengths that are more than three times longer than their diameters are easily stressed and broken. Some of the thinnest bits are milled into their shank, making them even more fragile. The ⅜-in.-dia. bit shown at left has less than ¹⁄₁₆ in. of steel between the flutes. Cut in ⅛-in. increments or less with these bits.

Trapped Bits Need Precise Guidance Some bit designs, such as dovetail bits and T-slot cutters, trap the bit in the work. The slightest wavering in the cut will mess up the workpiece. These bits should be used only with jigs and fences to guide them.

Dovetail and T-slot bits also break easily. They are designed to cut while fully engaged

in the workpiece, which is the most stressful kind of cut for any router bit. Most of the cutting is done at the ends of the flutes where their diameter is at a maximum. However, most of the stress is concentrated where the shank and the flutes meet, which is the thinnest part of the bit. To make matters worse, some of these cutters are ground into the shank. Just take things easy and don't force the cut. For long T-slots and sliding dovetails, I pre-plow with a straight bit.

Many other kinds of bits cut in such a way that you can't lift the router straight up and off the workpiece freely. These bits include cope-and-stick cutters, glue- and finger-joint bits, bullnose bits, and some profile bits. To be used successfully, they should be treated as trapped bits.

Spiral Bits Can Be Unpredictable Spiral up-shear and down-shear bits can produce impeccable surfaces. The cutting edges travel in a spiral motion and are always engaged in the work, unlike ordinary straight bits. Up-shear bits send the chips into your face, and down shears send the chips into your socks (see the photo above right).

Large spiral-ground down-shear bits have one nasty feature: If the bit catches in the work, it will pick the router up and out of the cut. I almost lost my grip on a router with a down-shear bit that suddenly climbed up the work. Down shears are too unpredictable for this woodworker, especially on end grain. If you use them, cut very lightly or use them in a router table with a power feed.

2. Listen to Your Router Whine

Routers always seem to whine, but you should listen to them. The sound a router makes while idling should not change appreciably in the cut. If it does, you may be stressing the bit and the motor.

It's all too easy to overwork a bit because it's difficult to estimate how much stress a particular cut will put on a bit. The volume of material you remove increases exponentially when you double the dimensions. This means that you remove 25 times more wood from a given length of a ⅝-in.-sq. rabbet than from a ⅛-in.-sq. rabbet. However, the stresses on the bit are not 25 times as great. Your best estimate will come from how it sounds in the cut. If your bit chatters, screeches, or just sounds unhappy, then slow down the cut.

3. Jigs Are Safety Devices in Disguise

Jigs secure the work and control the path of the cut, reducing the chances of error. Consequently, they are essential to the most accurate—and the safest—router cuts.

The best jigs have a few things in common. They secure the workpiece without interfering with the path of the router. They offer a large surface for the router to run on, giving it stability. And jigs guide the router positively and completely through the cut. Avoid designing jigs that trap the workpiece between a fence and the cutter. When using an edge guide on a router, position the bit in the fence.

A TWIST TO THE LEFT AND A TWIST TO THE RIGHT. The up-shear bit (left) spins like a drill bit, with the flutes spiraling up. The down-shear bit's flutes (right) spiral down.

A GOOD JIG KEEPS THE ROUTER IN LINE. By controlling the line of cut, jigs make mistakes less likely.

DIRECTIONS FOR CLIMB CUTTING

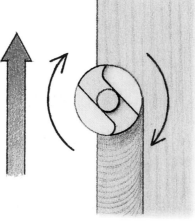

The drawing shows a climb cut. Though risky, routing in this direction produces a smooth surface.

DIRECTIONS FOR ANTI-CLIMB CUTTING

For the safest cuts, run the router counterclockwise around the workpiece and clockwise inside of a workpiece. Reverse this for the router table, because the router is upside down.

Rout counterclockwise along outside edge.

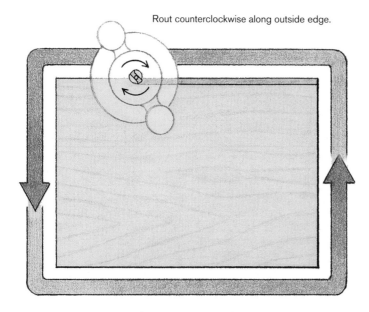

Rout clockwise along inside edge.

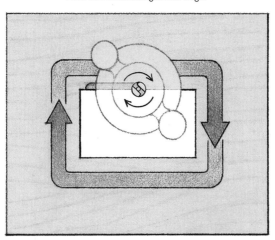

It's often the simplest jigs that help the most. On a standard outside edge cut, less than half the base casting rides on the workpiece. If you rout around a corner, as little as 25% of the base rides on the workpiece, and the chances of tipping are great. I make an offset subbase that increases stability by giving the router a larger platform to ride on.

4. Getting Away with the Climb Cut

The direction of cut has great bearing on the quality of the cut. If you look at a router upside down, you'll see that the bit spins counterclockwise, and when the router is on top of the workpiece, it's spinning clockwise. When the router is pushed through the cut with the bit spinning into the edge of the workpiece, it's called a climb cut (see the drawing at top left). The bit can self-feed or climb along the cut, wrenching the router forward. Running a router in the opposite direction, with the bit spinning out of the edge of the workpiece, is anti-climb cutting. Though riskier, climb cutting produces a superior edge, without the kind of tearout anti-climb cuts produce.

Use the anti-climb cut for most work, but when you need a perfect edge, use a climb cut, taking light passes. Learn to feel the speed and depth of cut when the router starts to grab and self-feed, so you don't lose control.

5. Keep Gravity on Your Side

Bad accidents with routers do happen. I heard of a carpenter who tried to rout some molding under a countertop. He did not secure the motor in the casting. Halfway through the cut, the motor spun out of its casting and onto his leg. The lesson should be obvious: Keep gravity on your side. Handheld routers should always

WRONG

RABBETING THE WRONG WAY. **Routing sideways can be tempting but is always treacherous. If you lose your grip, the router will fall.**

RIGHT

RABBETING THE RIGHT WAY. **The router is easier to control when flat on the workpiece. Your hands are above the bit if you lose your grip.**

be used horizontally with the bit facing down. It can be tempting to run a router sideways down a board, especially if the bit is oriented to cut that way, but don't do it. Find a different bit or make a jig that supports the piece in such a way that you rout horizontally (see the photos above).

6. Start the Router without Wobble

I start a router with its base casting flat on the edge of the workpiece. I find it troublesome and risky to set down an already running router on the workpiece. However, starting the router on an edge isn't completely risk free. Some machines will jerk from the torque of the motor and possibly push the bit into the workpiece. Worse, starting a cut before the bit reaches full speed can break the bit. I prefer soft-start machines because they don't twist on start up.

7. Rout Comfortably

Routing at a standard bench height is difficult and tiring for me. I can't see what's going on easily, so I end up hunched over trying to see where the bit is. Being able to see the bit is crucial to keeping the router under control. To solve the problem, I made a special routing bench 40 in. high. It allows me to stand tall and see what I'm

doing. I also make router jigs for my bench vise that stand at about the same height. I'm 6 ft. 1 in. tall, so 40 in. off the ground may not be the best height for you. Experiment to find your most comfortable routing height.

PAT WARNER is a woodworker and college instructor who lives in Escondido, California.

A SPECIAL ROUTER BENCH FOR COMFORTABLE WORK. **The author made this bench 40 in. high, so he doesn't have to lean over to see what he's doing.**

Routers for
Router Tables

BY PAT WARNER

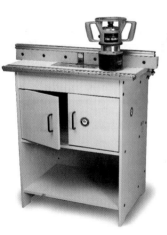

Although originally designed as a portable electric tool, the router performs just as well, if not better, as a stationary machine. Most of my routing is done with the tool attached to a small table made of medium-density fiberboard (MDF). Configured this way, the router can sometimes take the place of a shaper, a heavier-duty, more-costly tool that many of us can now do without.

Using the router inverted, however, poses some problems. The router was not designed for upside-down use. It's no surprise that most of the routers on the market are awkward to use in a table. I'm frequently asked what router works best in a table. Over the years I've tried just about every brand of router, and I can recommend five that work very well in a table.

Criteria for Choosing a Router

If you work fast or wish to use large panel-cutting bits, a large, powerful router is the way to go. Deeper cuts are possible with a 3-hp router. On the downside, a big router is also heavier and involves more of a wrestling match to get it out from under the table. So depending on the work you do, a 1½-hp or 2-hp machine might be all you need. I look for three essential criteria in a router to be used in a table.

1. The router should be easy to remove from its base. The easiest way to change a bit is by removing the router from its base and setting it on top of the table in plain view (see the photo on the facing page).

2. The router should have a ½-in. collet. A machine with a ½-in. collet can take heavier loads than a router with a ¼-in. collet. In addition, I prefer to use ½-in.-dia. shank router bits, which are also more durable and less prone to flexing under load.

3. The greater the range of depth adjustment, or travel, the more versatile the machine. Remember, the actual reach of a router will be minus the thickness of the tabletop to which it is attached.

Another feature worth considering—but it's not essential—is variable speed. If you plan to use 1½-in.-dia. or larger bits, go with a variable-speed machine. Otherwise, you won't get much out of this feature, which adds to the cost of the router.

For Heavy-Duty Use, I Rely on a 3¼-hp Router For heavy-duty router-table work, there is only one fixed-base machine that fits all of my criteria: the Porter-Cable® Speedmatic® 7518, a 3¼-hp, variable-speed machine. The 7518 also has the largest base,

GOOD TABLE MANNERS

These features make some routers better suited than others to be used as stationary tools:

1. Large-diameter mounting screws
2. Easy-to-read adjustment scale
3. Aftermarket locking lever
4. Lots of travel
5. $^1/_2$-in. collet
6. Detachable motor

the biggest base-plate screws, and the capacity to soak up more heat and run longer than any other router, fixed base or plunge. (Except for the variable-speed feature, it is similar to the Porter-Cable 7519.) The Porter-Cable motor has four pins that ride in matching spiral grooves cut into the base. Depth changes are made simply by spinning the motor up or down (see the bottom photo on p. 10). Minute depth-of-cut adjustments are easy to make using the

tool's adjustment scale (a large ring), which is marked off in $^1/_{64}$-in. increments.

Although the 7518 is tough enough to do raised panels in one pass, I generally take two or three passes when I have to remove a lot of material. Limiting cuts to the equivalent of about $^3/_8$ in. by $^3/_8$ in. at a time produces little tearout, and stock is easy to control when feeding by hand.

When routing upside down, a lot of fine dust can make its way into the spirals in the

The spring-loaded base of a plunge router is meant to be used right-side up, and it can be a struggle to make adjustments upside down. In addition, a plunge router cannot easily be removed from its base, which means you have to change bits with the tool attached to the table.

Midsize Routers For medium-duty work, I like the Milwaukee® 5680, Bosch® 1617, DeWalt® 610, and Porter-Cable® 690. To avoid straining the motor of a midsize router, I don't cut more than the equivalent of ¼ in. by ¼ in. in a single pass. The Bosch, DeWalt and Milwaukee routers have the greatest amount of travel. The Bosch and Porter-Cable machines also have the most friendly depth-adjustment systems, something you appreciate every time you use it.

The Porter-Cable 690 is designed along the same lines as its bigger brother (the 7518) and employs the four pins on the motor housing. An easy-to-read scale is graduated in ⅟₆₄-in. increments but is readable to ⅟₁₂₈-in. increments because of the wide spaces between graduations. Vertical travel is about 1¾ in.

Most routers employ a thumbscrew to lock the base to the motor. The Bosch 1617 is designed differently. It has a two-stage system, consisting of a pair of locking levers. A pull of the main lever loosens the motor. The spring-loaded second lever provides a coarse adjustment and prevents the motor from coming loose from the housing unless pressure is maintained while the motor is twisted. A screw dial allows for fine adjustment. The dial is graduated in

motor housings of Porter-Cable routers and cause them to jam. To avoid jams, after routing, screw the motor up, toward the tabletop to eject dust from the grooves. Then screw downward to remove the dust; if you encounter resistance, go back up, then down again.

I know many woodworkers use a large plunge router in a table, but I've yet to find one that's as convenient to use as the 7518.

DEPTH CHANGES MADE EASY. All fixed-base Porter-Cable routers have four pins protruding from the motor housing that engage with two spiral grooves cut into the wall of the base. An adjustment scale is graduated in ⅟₆₄-in. increments.

Five Routers That Fit the Bill

Although any router can conceivably be fitted to a table, these models excel at the task. A fixed-base router is preferable over a plunge router because the motor is easily removed from the base.

Bosch 1617 (2 hp)

Milwaukee 5680 (2 hp)

Porter-Cable 690
(1½ hp)

DeWalt 610 (1½ hp)

Porter-Cable Speedmatic 7518
(3¼ hp)

Sources

Reid Tool Supply Company

2265 Black Creek Rd.
Muskegon, MI 49444
www.reidtool.com
(800) 253-0421

both ¹⁄₆₄-in. and ¹⁄₁₀,₀₀₀-in. increments, with easy-to-read lettering. Travel is about 1⅞ in.

The DeWalt 610 has a rack-and-pinion adjustment mechanism. A dial on the end of the gear shaft is graduated in ¹⁄₆₄-in. increments, but the dial is very small, and the cursor mark, cast into the base, is rather wide, so you can't rely on these components for highly accurate adjustments. Rubbing white crayon on the numbers will improve readability; but for fine adjustments, make a trial cut and measure. The machine has 2¼ in. of travel.

The Milwaukee 5680 has a flat-head screw attached to the motor that prevents it from detaching from the base. I remove that screw for router-table work so that I can change bits with the motor out of the base. Use that screw as a guide when reassembling the router to the base. If there's not enough base wrapped around the motor, it may vibrate loose. The Milwaukee has a depth-adjustment scale, which is graduated in ¹⁄₆₄-in. increments. The black bars on the black dial are not as easy to read as some other routers that have white lettering on a black background.

There's one thing about the Milwaukee to be aware of: The motor housing has a spiral-cut groove, but that is for the adjustment scale only. The motor moves up and down in a straight line. Don't try to spin the motor to change depth as you would a Porter-Cable router. Because of its design, the depth adjustment is a bit awkward with the router inverted because the adjustment scale is really designed to work with the tool in the upright position. The Milwaukee has about 2 in. of travel.

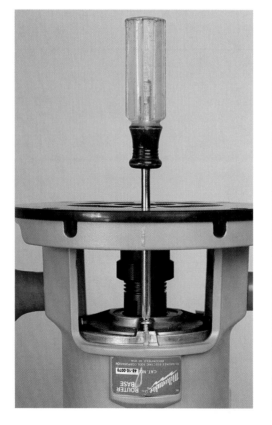

REMOVING THE MOTOR. **The Milwaukee 5680 router has a stop screw that must be removed to withdraw the motor from its base.**

THIS ROUTER HAS TWO ADJUSTMENTS. **The Bosch 1617 router has a lever (left) that allows for coarse adjustments and a screw dial for fine adjustments. The larger lever (right) locks the base to the motor.**

ANOTHER ADJUSTMENT SYSTEM. The DeWalt 610 has a rack-and-pinion adjustment system. The numerals on the depth-adjustment scale can be made easier to read by wiping them with white crayon or ink.

Router Safety and Maintenance

The potential for a router motor to eject itself accidentally from the base is always a possibility with a fixed-base router whether it's being used upside down or right-side up. This kind of accident is typically the result of not fully tightening the thumbscrew that fastens the base to the motor.

I've replaced the thumbscrews on some of my Porter-Cable routers with adjustable levers, which are easier to grip and allow greater locking forces. The levers (including the bronze sleeve and flange nut) cost less than $10 and are available from Reid Tool Supply Company. The holes in the base for the locking lever will have to be reamed or drilled out slightly to accept the larger-diameter replacement part. Also, a flat must be filed on the nut to fit it to the base, which will keep it from spinning freely when the lever is moved.

PAT WARNER is a woodworker and college instructor who lives in Escondido, California.

Why I Don't Like Base-Plate Inserts

When I started woodworking, the routers sold in the United States were all fixed-base machines. Router tables were still new, and there weren't lots of accessories, such as base-plate inserts, available. My router table consisted of a solid piece of stock. To change bits, I simply unscrewed the router motor from its base attached to the underside of the table.

I still prefer a solid router tabletop because a base-plate insert introduces its own problems. True, a base-plate insert allows you to use any type of router, including a plunge router, because the tool and base can be removed from the table to access the machine's collet. But I find it difficult to adjust a plunge router when it is turned upside down.

A base-plate insert compromises any router table. Cutting a big hole in a table invites twist and cup. An insert must be perfectly level to get a smooth transition from table to insert. In addition, some inserts themselves may bend under load.

I made a simple, inexpensive table from a piece of ⅝-in.-thick MDF (sealed on all faces and edges with three coats of Watco® oil). Sanding thickness tolerances of cabinet-grade MDF are very high (0.002 in. to 0.004 in.), which ensures a flat table. Instead of using insert rings to keep the opening around the bit to a minimum, make two or more tops with different size openings. Attach the MDF to a wooden table with several cross braces underneath to ensure that it stays flat.

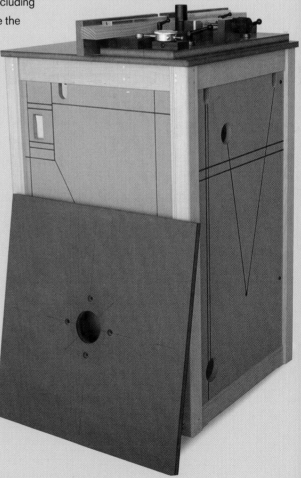

Tune Up Your Router

BY JOHN WHITE

In most shops a router gets plenty of hard work, so it's not surprising that an occasional problem can show up. But just because your router has been acting finicky doesn't necessarily mean it's time to replace it. You can often get it back into tip-top shape if you know where the problems are likely to be hiding. And chances are, the fix won't cost you much time or money.

As manager of the *Fine Woodworking* shop, I get to see quite a few routers. The problems that most of them have had can be distilled into one of three categories.

The main problem I see is related to the height-adjustment mechanism. Over time it may become difficult to adjust. Or it does not lock properly, causing the motor to creep out of position.

Second on my list of common problems has to do with the collet. Sometimes it won't grip the shank of the bit tightly enough, causing the bit to slip.

Worn brushes are the third most common problem. When brushes have worn too much, the motor might not start. If the motor does manage to run, it can unexpectedly cut out under load.

Height-Adjustment Problems

It's not unusual for the height-adjustment mechanism to stick or bind, especially on a

Plunge Perk-Up

It takes just a few simple steps to rejuvenate most any plunge router that is suffering from a balky height-adjustment mechanism.

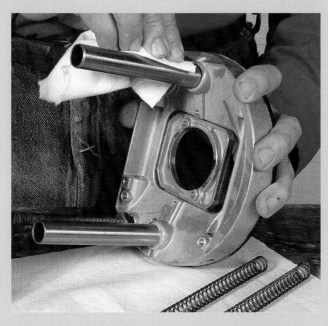

CLEAN THE POSTS. Remove the springs from the guideposts before cleaning the outside of the posts with WD-40.

SMOOTH OUT ANY BURRS. A burr on the guidepost can make for a sticky plunging action, so a little smoothing with a diamond stone could be in order.

WORK ON THE BORES. A cleaning stick, made from a piece of paper towel wrapped around a dowel, is used to clean out the holes that accept the guideposts.

BRUSH ON SOME GREASE. Give the springs a generous coating of lithium grease before reinstalling them in the guideposts.

Fixed-Base Fix-Up

A finicky height-adjustment mechanism on a fixed-base router can be smoothed out with a minimum of fuss.

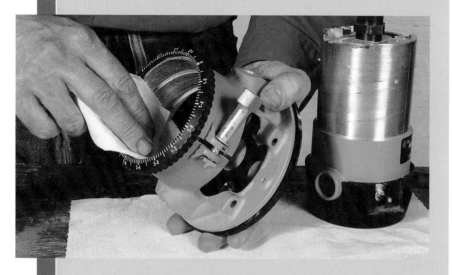

KEEP IT CLEAN. Wipe down the inside of the base and outside of the motor with penetrating oil, such as WD-40.

TAKE CARE OF YOUR TEETH. Some routers have a rack-and-gear mechanism. Any burrs on the teeth need to be smoothed with a needle file.

A MISALIGNED RACK-AND-GEAR MECHANISM WON'T OPERATE SMOOTHLY. Sometimes it takes just a few light taps from a hammer to realign the parts.

plunge router. When that happens, it's difficult to make precise adjustments. When the height adjustment is not working quite right, the first thing to do is check the sliding components and the lock mechanism. A buildup of grime prevents parts from sliding or meshing properly. And parts that aren't properly lubricated suffer the same problem. The fix here is simple enough. It's just a matter of cleaning and lubricating the parts.

Unfortunately, some routers have a complex lock or height-adjustment mechanism that makes disassembly difficult. In this case, first try cleaning and lubing without taking apart the router. Disassemble the machine only if you can't get it to free up.

On a plunge router, first remove the springs from the base unit. Then use a penetrating oil, such as WD-40®, and a paper towel or rag wrapped around a rod (a wood dowel works fine) to clean out the holes that accept the two guideposts. Then clean all of the old grease off the springs and wipe down the guideposts.

Use a paper towel or a rag wetted with WD-40 to get into the threads, grooves, gear tracks, and other nooks and crannies of the lock and depth controls of your machine. An old toothbrush also comes in handy here. Go over any moving or sliding parts, looking for burrs, rough spots, binding, and excess wear. Use files, stones, and emery paper to correct any problems you find.

Also examine the springs, nuts, and washers for burrs and distorted or worn-out parts. Washers especially can get cupped or chewed up, making the controls hard to work and lock handles difficult to tighten. If the router has a rack-and-gear mechanism, use a needle file to clean up any burrs down in the gear teeth that can cause interference.

On a fixed-base router, use a paper towel or rag wetted with WD-40 to clean the barrel of the motor and the inside of the base. Some fixed-base routers have a motor housing that threads into the base.

Clean the Collet

The collet grips the shank of the router bit. But it won't grip well if it isn't clean.

IF NECESSARY, REMOVE THE RING. Some collets are attached to the nut with a snap ring. External snap-ring pliers, sold by auto-parts stores, are used to remove the ring.

CLEAN OUT BURRS OR RUST. Use a dowel wrapped in 220-grit or finer emery paper to remove burrs or rust inside the collet.

MAKE SURE THE CENTER OF THE COLLET IS CLEAN. The inside of the collet grips the shank of the router bit. So after cleaning the collet, run several pieces of clean towel through the center of the collet to remove any residual oil or grit.

Make it a habit to clean out chips and saw-dust that get caught between the base and motor. Also, adding an occasional thin coat of wax to the sliding surfaces can reduce wear and help extend the life of the parts.

Eventually, these parts can wear to the point that it becomes hard to thread the motor or lock it in place. If you find that's the case, and if the base is metal, the most cost-effective fix is simply to replace the base. Little can be done for plastic routers because typically both the base and the body are worn out.

Now you can reassemble the machine, lubricating as you work along. Shafts and threads that are somewhat protected from sawdust can get a coat of light oil (such as sewing-machine oil) or lithium grease. On parts that get more exposure to sawdust, such as the guideposts or a sliding motor, it's best to use a stick lubricant or a good wax to make the parts slide smoothly.

Caring for the Collet

A typical router bit spins at 25,000 rpm. To prevent slippage, the collet on the router must maintain a viselike grip on the shank of the bit. So it makes sense to keep the collet in good working order. In time, grime can build up in both the collet nut and the collet, effectively reducing the squeeze on the shank. A collet that isn't properly lubricated can also have less grip-ping strength.

The nut and collet can also begin to wear or get distorted. And it doesn't take a lot of wear or distortion to cause problems. Indeed, a change of just a couple of thousandths of an inch can prevent the chuck from fully gripping the bit.

A collet that's worn or distorted can lead to vibration. And that could damage the shank of the bit or the inside of the collet. Or it can cause the bit to creep from the collet, changing the depth of cut as you rout. Should the bit creep far enough, the entire shank could come out in the middle of a cut—the woodworking equivalent of a nuclear meltdown.

Fortunately, it takes only a moment to make sure the surfaces of the collet are clean and properly lubricated. The proce-dure is pretty straightforward. Remove the router bit and unscrew the nut, then lift the collet from the spindle. On some routers, the nut stays attached to the collet.

Once the collet is out, you can blow out any sawdust. Also give a quick visual inspection to the taper inside the end of the spindle. The tapered surfaces should be smooth, almost polished. And the tapers should be straight, not worn into a bell shape.

Check the collet for cracks, which sometimes show up along the edge, partic-ularly on thin-walled collets. Replace the collet if you spot one. Any burrs or rust need to be smoothed out. I use a fine stone on the tapered surface. On the inside, emery paper (220 grit or finer) wrapped around a dowel works well.

It's important to use a light touch when using a stone or emery paper. The idea is to remove the rough spots without changing the shape of the parts. The collet must fit precisely in the spindle taper. Be sure to clean off any grit left by the emery paper or stones. The grit will cause rapid wear if not removed.

If you find that a bit has spun inside the collet, chewing up the bore, the collet should be replaced. This sort of damage cannot be fixed and will allow bits to slip, damaging their shanks.

If the spindle taper is chewed up, the router is probably due for retirement. On some routers, the spindle taper is a separate part that threads onto the end of the spindle. But it typically requires special tools to remove and replace it.

If the critical surfaces are in good shape, it takes just a few steps to clean and lube the parts. Slightly moisten the corner of a paper towel (or clean rag) with WD-40. Then wipe down the inside of the nut, the collet, and the inside and outside of the end of the spindle. After that, use your fingernail to get the towel into the threads on the spindle.

Before cleaning the outside of the collet, tear off a small piece of the oil-treated towel and use a thin dowel to force the towel through the bore of the collet. Because the bore is the part of the collet that actually grips the bit shank, you don't want to leave oil residue there. So run some pieces of clean towel through the bore to make sure all of the oil is gone.

Worn-Out Brushes Need Replacing

To produce high power in a light, compact package, a router uses a universal-type motor. Common to this motor is a pair of small carbon blocks, called brushes, that rub against the commutator, a part that spins with a surface speed of some 60 mph. These brushes eventually wear down. When they wear too much, the router starts to complain. So it's a good idea to check the

Replacing Brushes

A router with badly worn brushes won't run well. Replace the brushes before they start to cause problems.

ACCESSING BRUSHES FROM THE SIDE OF THE ROUTER. On a router with side access to the brushes, remove a cap, then simply pull out the brush (along with an attached spring and lead wire) from the motor housing.

ACCESSING BRUSHES FROM THE TOP OF THE ROUTER. Some routers need the top housing removed to get at the brushes. Use a paper clip shaped into a long hook to grab and remove each brush.

brushes once in a while. And replace them before they wear too much.

One sign of worn brushes is an increasing amount of sparking that can be seen through the air vents on top of the router. Another common symptom is a motor that cuts in and out under load, or one that intermittently fails to start.

Running a router with badly worn brushes for any length of time can damage the soft copper surface of the commutator. Once that happens, the replacement brushes are going to wear faster than they should. Or worse yet, the motor may be ruined.

There is no sure guideline for how often to check the brushes for wear. Most owner's manuals recommend a check every 50 hours to 100 hours of running time. But running time isn't easy to track, so I just check them once or twice a year.

So how do you know when a brush needs to be replaced? A few manufacturers mold a wear line on the brush. Once worn to the line, it's time for a new brush. Most of the time, however, the brush won't have a wear line. When that's the case, check whether the owner's manual tells you when to replace the brush.

If the manual isn't helping (and that's not uncommon), there's a pretty good rule of thumb that applies here: Replace the brush when it becomes shorter than it is wide. For example, a typical ¼-in.-thick by ⅜-in.-wide by ¾-in.-long brush (when new) should be replaced when it wears to ⅜ in. long. By the way, worn or damaged brushes should always be replaced in pairs.

Most router manufacturers have made brush changing a simple procedure. On many machines, you can reach the brushes by removing two dime-size plastic caps set 180° apart on the top of the machine. With the caps removed, the brushes will easily slide out of their brass housings. Brushes held in by threaded caps are typically bonded to a spring and lead wire.

Some routers have the brushes inside the plastic housing that covers the top part of the motor. Held on by a few screws, the cover is usually simple to remove, although some makers hide the screws under labeling that must be peeled off or cut. With the cover removed, the brush assemblies should be easy to spot. Most likely, they are going to be held in position by flat coil springs.

A paper clip comes in handy here. Straighten the clip and bend one end into a small hook. Slip the hook under the spring, then pull it back to release the brush. Be careful, though. The brush could shatter if the spring snaps back against it.

After checking the length of the brush, it's also a good idea to inspect its general condition. A bad electrical connection or heavy use can burn the brush, causing it to crack or crumble.

While you have the brushes out of the router, take a moment to look over the springs and lead wires that usually are attached to the back of the brush. On the springs, look for evidence of burning or cracking. And check the wire to see if it is frayed, broken, or even pulled out of the brush. Any one of these problems is a good reason to install fresh brushes.

Replacement brushes are typically available from the manufacturer. If they can't supply brushes because the motor is too old, a motor repair shop might be able to help. By the way, when installing new brushes, make sure they slide easily into their housings. If they don't, file them down as needed to get a good fit.

In addition to his work as a contributing editor, JOHN WHITE helps keep the *Fine Woodworking* shop in smooth running order.

All About Router Bits

BY JEFF GREEF

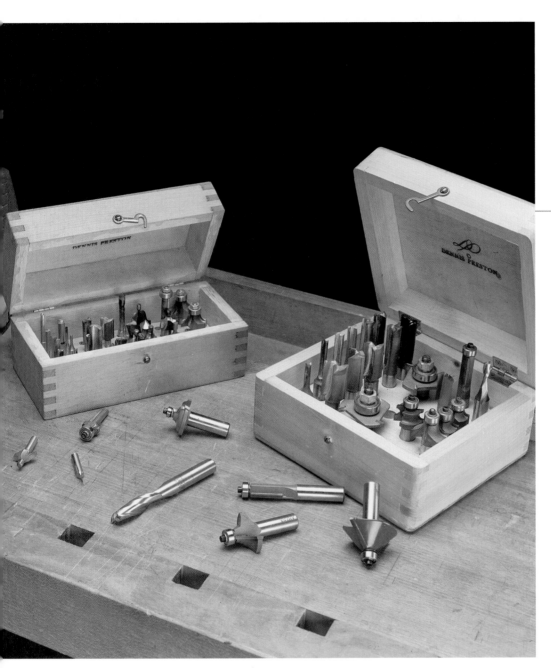

NO SHORTAGE OF CHOICES.
Router bits come in a variety of
profiles, materials, and sizes.
Storing them in a fitted box
helps protect edges and makes
bits easy to find.

For many woodworkers, a good-quality router may seem like an expensive tool. But few of us realize as we start to acquire tools that the cost of a router, or even several routers, pales in comparison to what we'll spend over time for bits. The growing selection of bits is what makes the router so versatile. They're capable of everything from molding edges to cutting raised panels. But with so much

to choose from, it's harder than ever to buy wisely.

It's surprising that a tool with roots in metalworking should become such an indispensable tool for woodworking. The router has no hand-tool counterpart—it's a milling machine.

Router and bit technology was transplanted first to industrial woodworking operations and then to the small shop. And

BOTH BITS MAKE A CUT ½ IN. WIDE, but the ½-in. shank (left) reduces chatter and allows a more aggressive cut than the ¼-in. shank bit.

SPIRAL FLUTE CUTTERS SLICE WOOD FIBERS. The down-shear bit (left) leaves a crisp edge at the top surface. The up-shear bit efficiently ejects chips.

industry is still the source of advances we see in bit design. At one time, for instance, carbide was an exotic material for industrial use only. Now it's more common than steel.

Similarly, new materials, coatings, and bit styles are slowly working their way into the mainstream. It's easy to amass a wallet-flattening, little-used collection. You have to weigh the bit's intended use as well as its cost and overall quality. The sidebar on pp. 24–25 gives suggestions on bits for specific cutting operations.

Carbide Stays Sharp Longer Than Steel

High-speed steel and tungsten carbide are the two most widely used materials in router bits. Steel is inexpensive, and because of its uniform crystalline structure, steel can take a keen edge and can produce a very smooth finish.

Steel bits may be the right choice for short runs or one-time operations. You can easily can sharpen flat-fluted steel bits and, with a grinder, modify the profile. But steel wears quickly, especially in highly abrasive

materials like plywood, medium-density fiberboard (MDF), and particleboard.

Tungsten carbide is an alloy of carbide granules and powdered cobalt fused under high pressure and temperature. The hardness of carbide is directly related to the amount of cobalt used—the smaller the percentage of cobalt binder, the harder the alloy.

But an extremely hard metal is brittle, too fragile for a cutting edge. So manufacturers strive for the best compromise between hardness and shock resistance. Because of extreme hardness, carbide holds an edge 25 times longer than steel. And although more expensive than steel, carbide is generally a better value.

Most carbide bits have carbide-cutting tips brazed to a steel body, combining the hardness of carbide and the economy and shock resistance of steel. Manufacturers also offer solid-carbide bits. These bits are much more expensive. But a solid-carbide bit has two advantages: It will withstand high temperatures generated by high feed rates and continuous use, and it's more than three times stiffer than steel so that chatter and

tip deflection are minimal. Sharpening carbide bits is more difficult than steel, but for minor edge touch-ups, a diamond honing stick can be used.

Polycrystalline diamond bits are now being advertised as the ultimate bit for highly abrasive man-made materials. A typical bit costs approximately $500 (which is 40 times more expensive than carbide but lasts 150 times longer). Users are large commercial manufacturers; but if history serves, we may someday see these bits in small shops.

Matching the Bit to the Job

How well a bit performs depends on factors like shank diameter, number of flutes (or cutting edges), shear angle of the cutter and type of pilot.

SHEAR ANGLE REDUCES TEAROUT ON END GRAIN. **The angled cutter on this rabbeting bit cuts cleanly in redwood.**

STRAIGHT BITS CHOP THE WOOD. **Bits without a shear angle cut cleanly with the grain but not as smoothly on end grain.**

Bits for Specific Cuts

Y ou'll get the best results by choosing a router bit specifically designed for the job. If the bit is to be used regularly, a bit with a ½-in. shank and high-quality carbide is a good choice.

—Dennis Preston, assistant editor of *Fine Woodworking*

PLUNGE MORTISING AND DADOES

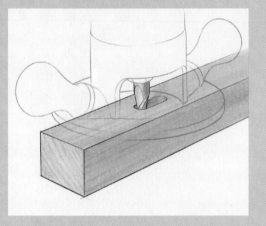

A spiral up-shear bit (left) is unmatched in its chip-clearing ability. These bits cut fast and clean with minimum chatter. When cutting into laminate or splintery wood, use a down-cut spiral to eliminate chipping at the top edge of the cut. It will be slow going, though, because you will have to stop frequently and blow the chips out of the cut.

CUTTING THROUGH STOCK WITH TWO GOOD SIDES

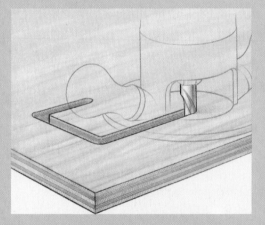

A compression bit (half of which is an up-shear and the other half a down-shear) is a specialty bit used when the edge of both upper and lower surfaces must be crisp. This bit design sacrifices feed rate and chip-clearing ability for unblemished edges.

MAKING ROUGH CUTOUTS THROUGH STOCK

A single-flute, stagger-tooth bit cuts aggressively and roughly. The tooth orientation minimizes chatter.

EDGE MOLDING AND RABBETING

A bit that has a slight shear angle cuts more smoothly. For freehand routing and following curves, a ball-bearing pilot is the easiest to use. An edge-guide attachment or a fence lets you use a bit that doesn't have a pilot.

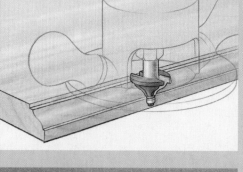

TEMPLATE AND PATTERN ROUTING

Flush-trimming or pattern-routing bits have a pilot bearing mounted on the shank, either above or below the cutting tips, and are used with a template to guide the bit. The top-pilot location has one big advantage over a bottom-mounted bearing: The template can be mounted above the work and the bit plunged into the work.

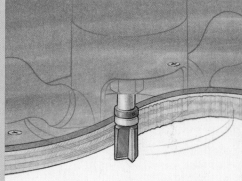

PANEL RAISERS

Large-diameter bits let you lay the stock flat on a router table. These bits generally produce a smooth finish. With them, you can easily follow curves. But these bits should be run at about 12,000 rpm, which is slower than most fixed-speed routers. Face molding, or safety raisers (shown in photo at left), can run at higher speeds but the stock must be held on edge against a fence. Molding a curved piece of stock is not easy.

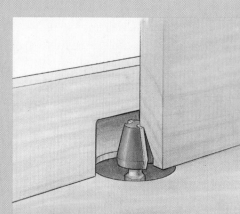

GROOVING FOR SPLINES AND BISCUITS

A slot cutter is really a small saw with a precise kerf width. You can mount cutters from 1/16 in. to 1/4 in. on a standard arbor. Some new sets allow stacking cutters like a dado set to get widths up to 11/16 in. Changing the diameter of the pilot bearing controls the depth of cut.

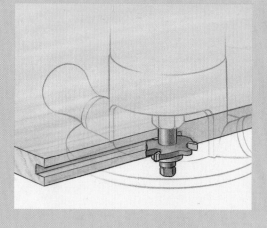

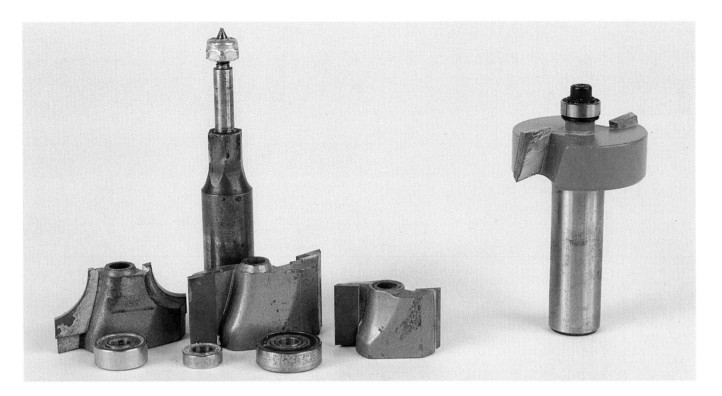

Use Largest Shank Diameter Shank diameter should correspond to cutter size (see the left photo on p. 22). Large bits need the stiffness of ½-in. shanks to minimize vibration and deflection. Many bits with small cutting profiles are available only with ¼-in. shanks. If you have a choice between a ¼-in. or a ½-in. shank, pick the larger one. The router's collet will grip better, and the extra mass minimizes chatter (the result of vibration and deflection) to produce a better cut. And select the shortest cutting edge that meets your needs, because excessive length increases vibration.

More Flutes for a Smoother Cut The gap, or flute, in front of the cutting edge provides clearance for chip removal. Most bits have two flutes, but some have one, three, or four. More flutes (and, therefore, more cutting tips) produce a smoother cut, but they reduce the feed rate the bit will allow. Conversely, a single-flute, straight bit works great for making rough cutouts in stock quickly.

Choose a Shear Angle That's Right for the Job Bits cut better when the cutting edge is angled slightly in relation to the centerline of the bit. This is called the shear angle. The effect is similar to skew-cutting with a plane or a chisel. Bits with no shear angle chop their way through the stock. The shear angle causes more of a slice than a chop, producing a smoother cut (see the bottom photos on p. 23). Most manufacturers I spoke with believe the difference is pronounced only on end-grain cuts.

The shear direction can be either up or down. Up-shear bits (the most common) quickly clear chips from the cut and tend to pull the router base down on the work. Down-shear bits are used where an upward cut would leave a ragged edge at the top surface. Down-shear bits make exceptionally clean cuts in veneered and laminate-covered surfaces. However, they do not clear chips well when mortising and tend to push the router base off the work.

Spiral bits take shear angle to the extreme. The helical flutes provide a continuous slicing action and are excellent at ejecting chips from the cut. They are especially well suited to mortising. For a more economical alternative, you can use two-flute, machinist's end mills (see the top photo on p. 23). These are cutting bits designed for machining metal, but they also cut wood. Like spiral bits, end mills have helical flutes and cut wood very well. The range of sizes is more limited than router bits, but they are inexpensive and are easily available at industrial tool-supply stores.

A note of caution when using up-shear spiral bits and end mills: the force developed by the high shear angle tries to pull the bit out of the collet. Be sure the collet and bit are in good condition, free of rust and burrs. The bit should be well seated, not bottomed out, in the collet, and the collet nut must be securely tighened.

Ball-Bearing Pilots Work Best for Edge Profiling

A pilot bearing, found on edge-trimming and edge-molding bits, guides the bit and limits the depth of cut (see the photo below). One-piece steel bits generally have a solid pilot, which is simply a small knob at the end of the shank that rubs against the edge of the work. Solid pilots work, but two problems can arise. If you don't keep the bit moving, the spinning pilot generates enough heat to burn black marks in the edge of the stock. And because of their small diameter, solid pilots can dig into the surface on which they ride, particularly on softer woods. That causes the cut to go slightly deeper than intended. Ball-bearing pilots take care of these problems. The large-diameter pilot bearing is unlikely to dig into the wood, and burning is eliminated because the bearing doesn't spin against the wood.

Arbors with Removable Cutters are Versatile

Bits come in two basic designs: those with cutters permanently attached to the shank body and those with separate cutters that attach to a threaded shank, or arbor, with a nut. When you want a different profile with an arbor and cutter set, all you do is change the cutter itself.

Bits with separate cutters are versatile and cost far less than buying a number of separate bits. I have one arbor on which I

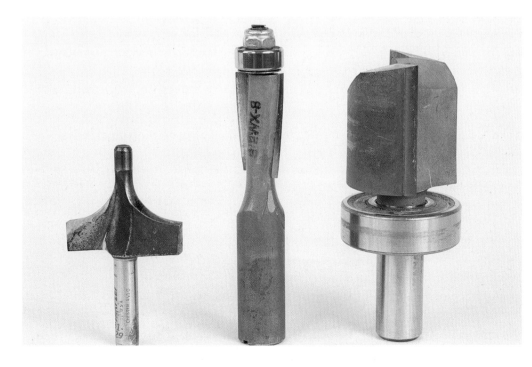

INTERCHANGEABLE PARTS ARE VERSATILE. A variety of cutters and pilot bearings can be mounted on one arbor, saving the cost of buying a number of single-purpose bits.

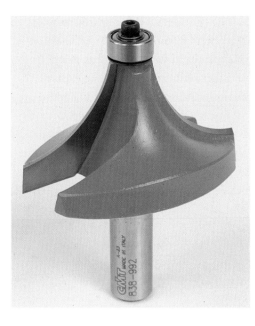

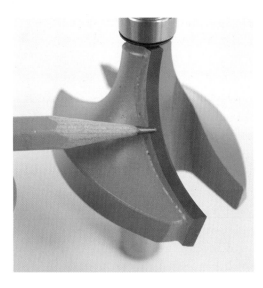

A PENCIL SLIDES EASILY along a smoothly ground edge. The lead is scraped away on a coarsely ground edge.

CHIP-LIMITING ANTI-KICKBACK DESIGN REDUCES THE BITE that the bit can take and prevents over-feeding.

can fit one of two rabbeting cutters with any of three different diameter pilot bearings (see the photo on p. 26). This gives me six different rabbet depths. Pilot bearings of different diameters often can be switched even on bits that do not have interchangeable cutters. The bearings change the depth of cut and expand the bit's usefulness. In fact, a slightly smaller diameter pilot bearing is the only difference between a beading and a roundover bit.

Replaceable Cutters and Special Coatings

Carbide insert tooling, long available in industry, lets you replace just the cutters when they get dull. A disposable cutting bit is fastened to the body with screws. Initially more expensive than fixed-cutter bits, insert tooling may be cheaper in the long run for heavy-use applications because the cutters are cheap to replace. Insert tooling offers a consistent cutting diameter or profile. The same can't be said for standard bits whose dimensions are altered by sharpening.

Brightly colored, Teflon® coatings are now widespread on several brands of bits. These coatings reduce pitch buildup and promote chip clearing.

In my work, I have not found this to be a big advantage, but colored bits do enhance safety. A spinning red or yellow bit is easier to see than a dull gray one.

The coating used on industrial metal-working bits, such as titanium nitride and zirconium nitride, are beginning to push into woodworking. Because these coatings are slippery, they withstand tremendous heat and promote faster chip clearing on very abrasive materials. The result is cooler cutting and longer tool life.

Anti-Kickback Designs Are Widely Available Most manufacturers now offer an anti-kickback design on their bits, which limits the amount of wood the bit can bite on each revolution (see the photo above left). This prevents overfeeding, which can cause kickback. Many manufacturers I spoke with believe this design is most useful on shaper cutters and on large router bits like panel raisers where kickback is a serious threat. The smaller bits, they said, don't present enough danger to warrant the design. I agree with them.

How to Spot a Quality Bit

Finish grinding is the most expensive process in bit manufacture and the most critical. A smooth cut requires a sharp edge, and a sharp edge requires a smooth face and edge. Technically, grinding faces smooth is easy; grinding edges is not, particularly on curved, pattern-shaping bits. I have seen wide variation in the smoothness of edge grinding on bits, and now it's the first thing I look for.

Take a pencil with you when buying a bit. Run the tip along the edge of the bit. If the tip scrapes along rather than slides smoothly, chances are the bit has been ground to a rough finish and will leave small nicks in the work (see the right photo on the facing page). A rough grind also causes the bit to dull faster because the minutely serrated cutting edge loses relatively big chunks of carbide granules.

Carbide tips must be brazed securely to the steel body or the brittle carbide can break loose and fly like shrapnel. Always inspect bits for brazing voids. Don't use any that appear unsafe. In industry, a general rule is to reject any bit with a void larger than a pinhole.

Many manufacturers I spoke with said that a visual inspection of a bit says a lot about its quality. If the brazing is splattered or a grinding wheel has touched a spot it shouldn't have, attention to detail was lacking. The presence or absence of any kind of warranty with a bit is probably a good measure of the manufacturer's confidence in its work.

Why are there such wide price differences in bits that look similar? Generally, it's because there are many manufacturing practices affecting quality that you can't see. There is no universal quality standard for rating carbide, and it all looks the same.

The care taken by the manufacturer when brazing the carbide to the body and grinding the edge may not be obvious. Yet these factors can affect the longevity of the material because overheating reduces carbide's ability to hold an edge. Some bit shanks are hardened, others are not. The quality of grinding on the shank itself determines how accurately the bit spins and cuts. All of these factors are reflected in the cost.

Choosing Bits and Building Your Collection

The most important factor to consider when deciding how much to spend on a bit is cost per cut. Many expensive bits are made to be used in commercial situations where the bits will be used to destruction. In the long run, it is more cost effective for commercial shops to buy the most expensive bits.

But if you won't be using a bit very much, it doesn't make sense to buy the most expensive one. A less-expensive bit might not hold up as long, but you may not use it enough to have it resharpened even once.

Many bit manufacturers and retailers offer boxed bit sets at lower prices. Before you buy one of these sets, though, seriously consider whether you will use more than half of them. The price break you get on the set may be substantial, but if you use less than half the bits, you will have spent more money than if you had bought only the bits you'll need.

Choose bits as you go according to the design and profile you need and the quality you want for that bit.

JEFF GREEF is a woodworker and writer in Santa Cruz, California.

Spiral Router Bits vs. Straight Router Bits

BY PAT WARNER

WHY SPIRAL BITS ARE BETTER FOR PLUNGE CUTS. Because a spiral bit is designed much like a drill bit, it makes plunge cuts easily. The cutters of a straight bit do not overlap, so if you plunge straight down deeper than ³⁄₃₂ in., you might burn away the wood in the middle, but you won't cut it.

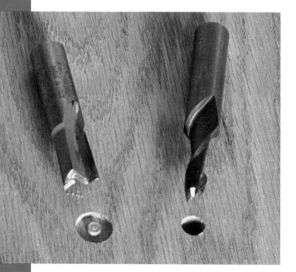

The increasingly popular spiral router bits borrow technology from the metalworking industry. Spiral bits look like drill bits and are most often made of solid carbide, so they are super sharp and leave a superior cut on wood. Two flutes ground around the body of a spiral bit smooth vibration by spreading the cutting action over a longer edge. With their drill-like point, spiral bits are also better for plunge-cutting. All of these advantages also mean less wear and tear on the router. But don't throw out all of your old straight bits just yet.

The new solid-carbide spiral bits come with some disadvantages. The first is that the cutters are expensive. A typical solid-carbide spiral bit is likely to cost at least $50. A similarly sized straight bit with carbide-tipped cutters will run somewhere in the range of $7 to $23. With a cost differential that large, you will want to know what you are going to do with this bit and that you will use it often enough to get your money's worth. To highlight other differences, let's compare the qualities of spiral bits and straight bits.

Both Spiral and Straight Bits Have "Plunge-Ability"

You can plunge with both types of bits, so they'll both work for, say, cutting mortises. But because most spiral bits are ground on the tip end of the flute, somewhat like a drill, you can plunge straight down as far as you like, without stopping. You can't really plunge any deeper than about ⅛ in. with a typical straight bit. Inspect the end, and you'll see why (see the photo at left). On most straight bits there is a space above the web, between the cutters, where no cutting takes place during a straight plunge because there is no cutter overlap. Chuck a straight bit into your drill press and plunge it into a piece of wood. After about ³⁄₃₂ in., the middle of the bit bottoms out. To go any farther, the bit has to abrade the wood away in this middle area.

This doesn't mean you can't cut mortises or plunge with a straight bit. You just have to sweep the router while you are plunging. You should probably cut mortises in passes not much deeper than ⅛ in. anyway, but with a straight bit, such shallow passes are just about a must.

Spiral Bits

ADVANTAGES

- Very clean cut
- More cutter in wood means less vibration
- Better plunge-cutting
- Less wear and tear on router
- Direct chips up or down

DISADVANTAGES

- Limited lengths and diameters
- Can be somewhat risky to use

Straight Bits

ADVANTAGES

- Wide variety of lengths and diameters
- Guide bearings on tip or shank mean better template routing
- Less expensive
- Greater ability to resharpen

DISADVANTAGE

- Plunge-cutting requires more effort and skill

THERE'S NO CLEAR WINNER. Solid-carbide spiral bits are becoming increasingly popular because they make a very clean cut. But they have many limitations compared to the straight bits that have been popular for years.

DIFFERENT CUT,
DIFFERENT SPIRAL CUTTER

All spiral bits make clean cuts. This veneered plywood shows the effects of the three types of spiral bits on the top and bottom edges.

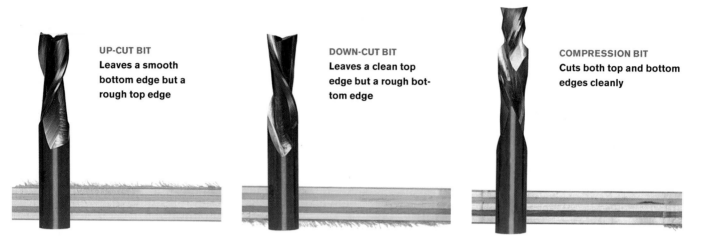

UP-CUT BIT
Leaves a smooth bottom edge but a rough top edge

DOWN-CUT BIT
Leaves a clean top edge but a rough bottom edge

COMPRESSION BIT
Cuts both top and bottom edges cleanly

Spiral Bits Leave a Clean Edge

The three basic cutter configurations for spiral bits are up-cut, down-cut, and a combination of the two, known as a compression bit. (For more on distinguishing between up-cut and down-cut bits, see the sidebar on p. 33.) A down-cut bit sends the chips downward; an up-cut bit sends them toward the shank. (On a router table, all directions are reversed.)

Besides directing the chips, the advantages of these configurations are best illustrated by the quality of cut, especially on veneered plywood (see the photos above). A down-cut bit will leave a clean edge on top but a ragged edge on the bottom; an up-cut bit will accomplish the opposite. This is great until you want to cut a dado with no tearout on the face. A down-cut bit will leave a clean top edge, but it sends the chips downward, into the dado where they have no place to go. You can make this cut, but you have to take it slower than usual to give the chips a chance to clear.

For woodworkers who work with A-grade veneers on both sides of the stock and must have a clean edge top, bottom,

and middle, the compression bit is a good choice. It has an up-cut configuration on the tip of the bit and a down-cut spiral ground on the shank. By lining up the bit just right, you can get a superior edge across the entire thickness of the wood. This virtuosity comes at a hefty price: A typical compression bit will cost about $90.

Straight Bits Come in Many Sizes and Bearing Configurations

Router-bit manufacturers have difficulty making solid-carbide spiral bits with cutting diameters larger than their shanks. So for small-shop hand routers you won't find many bits with a cutting diameter larger than ½ in., the size of the largest bit shank. Spiral bits also come pretty much in a few standard fractional sizes up to ½ in. Straight bits, on the other hand, go through dozens of fractional sizes, all the way up to 2-in.-dia. cutters. Depending on the job you have in mind for your router bit, straight bits also come in a variety of cutter lengths. So you can buy close to exactly the length of cutter you need.

Straight bits also have a huge advantage over spiral bits when it comes to template routing, because you can buy them with guide bearings. And those bearings can be mounted on the tip of the cutter or on the shank of the cutter, depending on your needs and your template. The bearings are made for a variety of cutter diameters and lengths. It is really too bad that solid-carbide spiral bits can't accommodate bearings a little more readily. With their superior edge cut, spirals make great template cutters when used with collar guides.

But when it comes to bearing-guided bits, spirals seem to be available only with bearings mounted on the end of the bit. There are some problems with this: The cost is high (about $80); it precludes cutting only partway through the work, which means full-thickness cuts only; and the template has to be under the work, an inconvenience. Shank-shod, bearing-guided, solid-carbide bits (spiral bits with the bearings on the shaft end of the bit), which would permit template routing with the template on top of the work and trim cutting through only part of the work face, are not available. For this type of routing, you'll have to stick with straight bits.

Sharpening Spiral Bits Is Difficult, if Not Impossible

Some woodworkers like to sharpen their straight bits, although I find it difficult to get it right and always send out my bits for sharpening. Carbide-tipped straight bits usually have enough carbide thickness to be reground four or five times, and the technology to do so is common.

A few services claim to be able to sharpen spiral bits. But I haven't found anyone who can sharpen spiral carbide to factory standards. To me, this translates into a substantial loss. Here's why: The spiral bit costs twice as much—or more—as a straight bit, and the straight bit can be reground up to five times. A sharpening service charges about

How to Tell an Up-Cut Bit from a Down-Cut Bit

Let's say you have an up-cut spiral bit and a down-cut spiral bit on your cabinet shelf but haven't used them in a while. How can you tell quickly which is which?

First, look at the right side of the bit (it doesn't matter whether the tip is facing up or down). Look at what direction the flute is heading as it goes around to the back side. If the flute is moving up as it curls around the right side of the bit (as in the bit at left in the photo), you are looking at an up-cut bit.

For a second test, hold the bit in your hand with the tip pointed down and away from you. Turn the bit in a clockwise rotation and watch the reflection of any light on the bit. If the light moves up the bit as you turn it, you are holding an up-cut bit. The light will move downward on a down-cut bit.

UP-CUT BIT   DOWN-CUT BIT

DOWN-CUT SPIRAL BITS ARE GREAT FOR DADOES, BUT GO SLOW. **Cross-grain dadoes can be cut with a down-cut bit (above right) or an up-cut bit (above left). The down-cut bit leaves a better surface, but you have to move more slowly to give the chips time to clear out of the cut.**

$4 to regrind a straight bit, and the cutter often comes back sharper than it was from the factory. So even if I pay $23 for a straight bit and sharpen it five times, I still pay only $43. Spiral bits might stay sharp longer than straight bits, but even so, the cost of using spiral bits will always be higher.

Spiral Bits Can Be Risky to Use

Spiral bits work incredibly well in the production environment and especially in CNC (computer numerically controlled) router industrial applications. But in a hand router, their use sometimes imposes unusual risks not associated with the equivalent or bigger straight bits. The down-cut spiral bit's screw-driven forces are sufficient enough to pick the router up and twist it out of your hands—with no warning. I know, because it has happened to me. On end grain the spiral bit is getting even more traction, so the risk is even greater—a pity, too, because a sweet end-grain finish is attractive.

The up-cut spiral bit can have the opposite effect. It wants to pick up the work. So you must secure the work in some kind of fixture or hold it by a clamp. (I never rout anything that is not secured or clamped, but some people do.) The up-cut bit's tendency to pick up the work also happens quickly and without warning.

My teaching and woodworking are centered on routing, so I have a cabinet filled with more than the weekend woodworker's supply of router bits. I do keep a few solid-carbide spiral bits because, when I want a beautiful face cut or I am cutting narrow mortises, and I have the money, there is just nothing better. But my cabinet is mostly full of a wide variety of straight bits. For general-purpose work, for template and pattern routing, and for those times when I need a large-diameter bit, I still reach for one of my straight bits.

PAT WARNER is a woodworker and college instructor who lives in Escondido, California.

Pick the Best Bit for the Job

A CLEAN SWEEP. Because of its plunging ability, a spiral bit is great for cutting mortises. You can plunge straight down, then move laterally. To plunge-cut mortises with a straight bit, you must plunge and sweep at the same time.

FOR PATTERN ROUTING, STRAIGHT BITS HAVE THE RIGHT BEARING. It is diffi-cult if not impossible to find spiral bits with bearings for pattern routing, whereas straight bits are available with bearings on either the shank (at near left) or cutter (at far left).

Router Bits Tackle Cope and Stick

aking frames with molded edges for glazed or raised-panel doors like the one in the photo below is a lot easier now that there are specialized stile-and-rail router bits on the market. But there are over 50 bit sets to choose from. To sort through this wide array of offerings, I obtained bits from 16 suppliers and manufacturers and put them through their paces. My objective was to find the real differences between bits and to provide guidelines for choosing a set. I inspected each set closely, scrutinizing for quality by eye. Then I tried out each set on pine, poplar, and oak to check the cut and the fit of the joints they produced.

BY JEFF GREEF

Deciphering the Differences between Dozens of Cutters

Stile-and-rail bits cut two profiles: a stick profile and a corresponding cope cut. The stick is the contour on the inside edges of a

YOU DON'T NEED A SHAPER for cope-and-stick joinery anymore. Now the market is teeming with router bits in a variety of styles competing for your cope-and-stick business.

SOLID BIT SETS LIKE THESE
COME IN PAIRS. **They have cutters that cannot be removed
from the shank.**

door or window frame on both the vertical members (stiles) and the horizontal ones (rails). The cope is a negative version of the stick and is cut into the ends of the rails, so they fit over the stick on the stiles, as shown in the drawing on the facing page.

All the stile-and-rail bit sets I examined cut a tenon and open mortise joint in addition to the cope and stick. The open mortise is the last few inches of the groove that also holds the panel. This joinery is adequate for small- and medium-size cabinet doors. You can beef up the joint with dowels or loose tenons in open mortises. Also, with some bits, you can make a rabbet for glass instead of a groove for a panel. If you make the glass rabbet, use a reinforcing joint because the tenon-and-open mortise joint is eliminated.

Solid Bit Sets Cope-and-stick bit sets come with solid bits or stacking bits. The cutters on solid sets cannot be removed from the shank for shimming or reconfiguration. As a result, the quality of the fit of cope to stick is entirely a function of how the bits are ground. Solid bit sets have two bits, one for sticking and one for coping, as shown above. The main advantage of solid sets is ease of use. You just chuck 'em up and go. The main drawback is lack of adjustability. If you get a set that gives a good fit, you'll be fine; but if not, you're stuck.

Sharpening is another consideration with solid sets. Carbide router bits are sharpened by grinding the flat face of the carbide. When the face is ground, the profile changes slightly as the cutting edge recedes along the bevel of the edge grind. Consequently, the fit of cope to stick

changes a little, too. Because there is no adjustment with solid sets, you can't compensate for these changes.

A solid set would be a possible choice for someone who is willing to sacrifice precision for ease of use and doesn't intend to use the bits enough to require resharpening.

Stacking Two-Part Like the solid types, two-part bits come in pairs, one bit each for coping and sticking (see the photos on the facing page). But with these bits, the slot cutters and profile cutters are separate and can be removed from the bit shank. This allows you to place shims between them to adjust the fit of the joint. The shims, provided by all manufacturers, are thin washers that fit over the shank. Shims won't cure all mismatches but should take care of 90% of them.

Two-part stacking bit sets are among the most costly of all stile-and-rail sets. And there is more set-up time because you must adjust the fit with shims when making test-cuts. But once the bits are properly shimmed and set up in two router tables, you never have to change setups. For any production situation where the bits would be used a lot, a stacking two-part set is the logical choice.

Stacking Reversible Unlike all the other bit sets, which come with mating pairs of cutters, stacking reversable sets use a single bit to cut both the cope and the stick. After cutting the copes, you remove the cutters from the bit arbor, and rearrange them to cut the stick. Just like the stacking two-part sets, reversible sets are adjustable with shims, as shown in the top photo on p. 40.

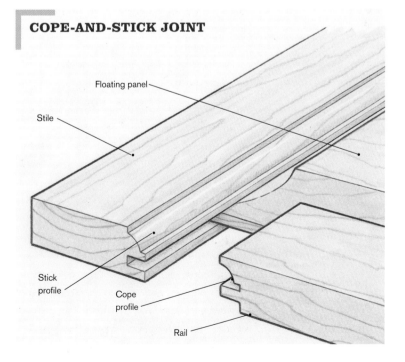

STACKING TWO-PART BIT SETS are paired and have removable cutters that can be restacked and shimmed for fit. Some have the anti-kickback design shown in the inset photos.

These sets cost less because you buy only one cutter assembly instead of two. But they won't last as long between sharpenings as a two-part set because the cutters in a reversible set do twice as much work.

If you want adjustability and you plan to make only a few doors, I would consider the reversibles because they cost less than two-part sets and their results are just as good. If you make a lot of doors, though, the constant need to switch a reversible set between cope and stick would become irritating.

The reversibility of these bits, while making them inexpensive and convenient, limits the range of possible profiles because a single cutter must shape both the cope and the stick.

Hybrid With hybrid bit sets, you use a separate cutter for each part of the joint (see the photo on p. 39). You make separate setups for each of the sticking, coping, grooving and tenoning passes. This can be tedious, but there are no shims to fuss with, and there is wide adjustability. And hybrids let you vary stock thickness. All the previously mentioned cutters are designed for specific stock thicknesses, usually ¾ in. Hybrid sets are the logical choice for special applications where you need to use odd stock thicknesses or for panel grooves that are wider than the standard ¼ in.

Architectural Architectural sets are designed specifically for making architectural windows and doors. The cutters are stackable and come in both reversible and two-bit sets, as shown in the photo on p. 41. Cutting standard architectural stock at thicknesses of 1⅜ in. or 1¾ in. with such bits

will require either a 3-hp router or multiple passes with a less-powerful machine.

Which Bits Are Best?

Once you've narrowed your search to a particular type of bit set, there are a number of factors to consider in choosing among bits. They run from the purely objective—price and specifications—to more subjective considerations. I've compiled data from my review of the bits in the chart on p. 38, and I'll explain what I looked for and why. When you buy bits, keep in mind that quality varies from bit to bit even from the same manufacturer. Examine bits closely, and return any that aren't up to snuff.

Grinding Quality You need a sharp edge on the carbide to get a smooth surface on the wood. Both the face and edge of the

COPE-AND-STICK JOINT

Floating panel

Stile

Stick profile

Cope profile

Rail

COPE-AND-STICK ROUTER BIT SETS

Manufacturer/Supplier	Country of Manufacture	Manufacturer's Stock Number	Price	Stock Thickness✳	Profile Type	Profile Depth✳	Shank Diameter✳	Fit of Cope and Stick	Quality of Edge Grind
Solid Bits									
Carb Tech®	Taiwan	AY12	$69.95	¾	Ogee	⅜	½	Cope good; tenon loose	Below average
Hartville	Taiwan	83641	$65.00	¾	Bead	⅜	½	Excellent	Average
MLCS	Taiwan	849	$74.95	1 (min.)	Step ogee	½	½◆	Very good	Below average
SY®	Taiwan	C1393	$99.95	¾	Round	¼	½	Cope good; tenon loose	Below average
Woodtek®	Taiwan	821026	$74.95	1 (min.)	Step ogee	9⁄16	½◆	Cope good; tenon loose	Below average
Stacking Two-Part Sets									
Bosch	U.S.A.	85625M	$133.40	¾	Ogee	⅜	½	Fair	Best
CMT®	Italy	891-502	$129.00	¾	Round	9⁄16	½	Excellent	Best
DML	U.S.A.	02024	$150.00	¾	Round	⅜	½	Excellent	Best
Eagle	U.S.A.	185-0900	$99.99	¾	Bead	⅜	½◆	Excellent	Average
Freud®	Italy	99-261	$153.00	¾	Ogee	10mm	½	Good	Best
MLCS	Taiwan	843	$74.95	¾	Round	⅜	½◆	Excellent	Below average
Porter-Cable	U.S.A.	43550 & 51	$144.00	¾	Bead	¼	½◆	Good	Average
Whiteside	U.S.A.	6002 A & B	$126.00	¾	Ogee	⅜	½	Excellent	Average
Stacking Reversible Bits									
Amana	Israel	55350	$117.60	¾	Ogee	⅜	½	Very good	Best
Eagle	U.S.A.	184-0105	$59.99	¾	Ogee	⅜	½◆	Excellent	Below average
F.S. Tool℠	Canada	FRB27	$109.00	¾	Ogee	12mm	½	Excellent	Best
Grizzly®	Taiwan	G2926	$49.95	¾	Step ogee	½	½◆	Excellent	Below average
Hartville	Taiwan	82141	$39.00	¾	Ogee	⅜	½	Excellent	Average
MLCS	Taiwan	894	$69.95	¾	Ogee	⅜	½◆	Very good	Below average
SY	Taiwan	C1654	$49.95	¾	Step ogee	⅜	½	Fair	Below average
Velepec	U.S.A./Israel	ROSRA-90-8	$110.00	¾	Ogee	⅜	½	Very good	Below average
Whiteside	U.S.A.	6151	$69.95	¾	Ogee	⅜	½	Excellent	Below average
Woodtek	Taiwan	820739	$37.50	¾	Step ogee	⅜	½◆	Fair	Below average
Hybrid Bits									
Freud	Italy	99-060&062✚	$60.00	Unlimited	Step ogee	½	½	Good	Best
Velepec	U.S.A./Israel	3-piece set	$140.00	Unlimited	Ogee	⅜	½	Good; very small gap	Below average
Architectural									
Amana	Israel	55340	$156.45	to 1¾	Ogee	¼	½	Excellent	Below average
Freud	Italy	99-050 & 051	$96.00	to 1¾	Ogee	6mm	½	Excellent	Best
MLCS	Taiwan	893	$54.95	to 1¾	Ogee	¼	½◆	Very good	Below average
SY	Taiwan	C1552	$89.00	to 1¾	Bead	5⁄16	½	Good	Below average

✳Inches, except where noted.   ◆Also available with ¼-in. shank.   ✚Two-piece set.

Smoothness of Cut	Comments
Below average	
Average	Burning; insufficient back grind
Average	Burning; insufficient back grind
Below average	
Average	Burning; insufficient back grind
Best	Without shims, bearing sparks against cutter
Best	Anti-kickback design
Best	
Average	
Best	Anti-kickback design
Best	
Average	
Average	
Average	
Below average	
Best	
Below average; small nicks	
Average; small nicks	
Best	
Below average; small nicks	Out of balance; cutters not ground at equal radii
Best	
Below average	
Below average; small nicks	
Best	
Best	
Average	Vibration
Average	Anti-kickback design
Average	
Below average; small nicks	

carbide must be ground smoothly. I found all bits had smooth face grinds. The major variable was the quality of the edge grind. I evaluated edge grinds by running a pencil tip along the carbide to see whether it slid smoothly or scraped along. Then I examined the stick each cutter produced, looking for nicks in the cut. Generally, I found bits with the best edge grinding left the best finish cuts.

Back Grind Another critical aspect of grinding is the angle of back grind. In back-grinding, the edge is ground at a sharp enough angle that only the very point touches the wood; the portion behind the edge should not. Without that clearance, burning will result. The heat can ruin the carbide, not to mention the workpiece.

Cutter Balance If bits are not balanced, they will vibrate while in use. I checked for mismatched cutters with the bits in the router. With the router unplugged, I held a steel rule on the router table and spun the bit. When the end of the rule just scraped one cutter, I spun the bit around to see how the other side compared. This technique will show only gross deviations from proper grinding indexing but is worth using whenever you chuck up a new bit or if an old bit is cutting poorly or with excessive vibration.

The Fit of Cope to Stick Fit depends on two factors. The first and most important is how well the manufacturer ground the cutters so that the cope is an exact match for the stick. The second is how well you set up the adjustments (when possible) to make the matching parts align. You can produce ill-fitting joints

Sources

*Amana Tool® Corp.
120 Carolyn Blvd.
Farmingdale, NY 11735
(800) 445-0077

*Bosch–SB Power Tool Co.
P.O. Box 12217
New Bern, NC 28562
(800) 334-5730

Carb-Tech®– Trend-lines
375 Beacham St.
Chelsea, MA 02150
(800) 767-9999

CMT
5425 Beaumont Center Blvd., Suite 900
Tampa, FL 33634
(800) 531-5559

*DML–Primark Tool
715 East Gray St.
Louisville, KY 40210
(800) 242-7003

Eagle America®
P.O. Box 1099
Chardon, OH 44024
(800) 872-2511

Freud
218 Feld Ave.
High Point, NC 27264
(800) 334-4107

*FS Tool
P.O. Box 510
Lewiston, NY 14092
(800) 387-9723

(Sources continued on p. 41.)

REVERSIBLE SETS USE ONE BIT TO CUT BOTH SIDES OF THE JOINT. The cutters can be shimmed to fine-tune the fit of cope to stick.

with well-ground cutters if you don't shim properly. But no amount of shimming will fill gaps in joints made with poorly ground cutters.

Solid cutters are not adjustable, so how well the joint fits is up to the manufacturer. Of those I tested, all had good matches of cope to stick, but several had poor fits of the tenon in the groove. The fits varied with different types of wood, which is common because router bits are ground at an angle that is a compromise between the optimum rakes for cutting hardwoods and softwoods.

Anti-Kickback Design The Italian bits (Freud and CMT) are well-made and impressive looking with their anti-kickback design that limits the depth of cut, reducing the danger of kickback and severe injury (see the inset photos above). Most technical

VOIDS IN THE BRAZING behind the carbide cutter can compromise the safety of a bit. The wire in the photo points to a void that is larger than the pinhole most manufacturers permit. But because it's within the diameter of the guide bearing, it's not likely to cause a problem.

A DEFECTIVE SHANK like this one, left rough on one side, can cause serious vibration. Remove the cutters to inspect a new bit before running it.

representatives I spoke with thought this feature was a good idea on larger-diameter cutters, such as panel raisers for which kickback is a serious threat, but overkill on smaller bits like these. I tend to agree.

Price and Value Why are there such wide price variations between bits of the same type? There are a number of factors that affect the quality and price of bits: different grades of carbide, types of brazing and brazing material, various edge-grinding and shank-grinding techniques. But it's difficult for the consumer to ascertain by observation or inquiry which materials and techniques were used to make a particular bit. I talked to Steve Cash, who runs a sharpening service here in Santa Cruz and sees thousands of bits a year. He said that, roughly speaking, higher price reflects the use of more expensive materials or processes in manufacturing.

In selecting for price, look for the lowest cost per cut. If you do a lot of cope-and-stick work, it makes sense to spend the money for a higher priced bit that will cut cleanly for a long time. If you have just a few doors, buy a less expensive bit. You may have to do some touch up sanding behind the bit, but you'll still come out ahead.

Personally, I think the best values among cope-and-stick bits are the reversibles. Because you're only paying

ARCHITECTURAL BIT SETS WILL TACKLE FULL-SIZE WINDOWS AND DOORS. **They come in both paired and reversible sets.**

for one shank, the prices are considerably lower than for two-part bits of comparable quality. Unless I knew I'd be in a production situation, I'd accept the extra toil involved in changing setups and get reversibles. The solid bits, though they seem like a bargain, didn't impress me with their performance. They were the only bits I tried that burned, and I also dislike their lack of adjustability.

Defective Bits

When you have your new bits, take a close look at them before putting them to use. Defective bits are not unheard of, and some potential problems will be evident on visual inspection.

Brazing Voids The brazing between a router bit's carbide cutter and steel body attaches the cutter to the body, and it acts as a cushion that protects the brittle carbide from fracturing under impact. Wherever there are gaps in the braze line, the possibility of fracture increases. If the carbide breaks while the bit is spinning, the result can be like shrapnel. The consensus among the manufacturers I spoke with was that nothing larger than a pinhole void in the brazing was acceptable. But the location of the void is important, too. The bit in the top photo had a void larger than a pinhole, so I sent it to Jim Effner for expert evaluation. (Effner is a former technical services engineer with Leitz, the German manufacturer of cutting tools, and is the author of *Chisels on a Wheel*, a book about motor-

driven cutters.) He said that because the void was at the small diameter of the cutter and within the span of the guide bearing, it wouldn't get much stress and wouldn't pose a problem.

Misground Shank I learned my lesson about carefully inspecting bits from experience. One bit that looked fine at first vibrated so much when I started it up that I immediately shut off the router. When I removed the cutters from the shank and looked closer, I found that half the upper shank was rough and unground, as shown in the bottom right photo on the facing page. In addition to checking for this type of defect, look at the lower section of a bit's shank. For the collet to grip it properly, the shank should be polished smooth and be free of blemishes.

It's Not the Bit, It's the Collet While you're paying all this attention to your bits, don't forget that they're in a partnership with your router's collet. Collets take a lot of abuse, and if they start to become egg-shaped, through wear or metal fatigue, they'll cause problems with your bits. According to Jim Effner, collets have a fairly predictable life span of 1,000 hours of use. So keep track of their birthdays, and replace them before they get too ancient.

JEFF GREEF is a woodworker and writer living in Santa Cruz, California

Sources

Grizzly
P.O. Box 2069
Bellingham, WA 98227
(800) 546-9663

Hartville Tool®
940 West Maple St.
Hartville, OH 44623
(800) 345-2396

MLCS
Box 4053 C13
Rydal, PA 19046;
(800) 533-9298

*Porter-Cable
4825 Highway 45 N.
Jackson, TN 38305
(800) 321-9443

SY–Cascade Tool Co.
Box 3110
Bellingham, WA 98227
(800) 235-0272

*Velepec
71-72 70th St.
Glendale, NY 11385
(800) 365-6636

***Whiteside
Machine Co.**
4506 Shook Rd.
Claremont. NC 28610
(800) 225-3982

**Woodtek®–
Woodworker's
Supply℠**
1108 North Glenn Rd.
Caspar, WY 82601
(800) 645-9292

* These companies do not sell directly to the public but will tell you who their local distributors are.

Spline Joinery

BY STEVEN COOK

In 20 years as a professional woodworker, churning out cabinets, making custom furniture and even some musical instruments, I've always looked for ways to make my two-man shop productive and profitable. One technique I use in virtually all my work is the spline joint.

The spline joint is simply the joining of two boards with a piece of scrap plywood or hardwood that's set into grooves routed in the two boards. Whether you need to align boards to be joined for a large tabletop, make face frames for a set of cabinets

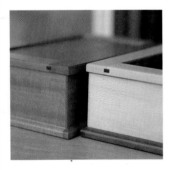

SPLINES CAN BE USED AS A DECORATIVE ELEMENT in addition to their structural role, as is the case with the ebony splines in the lids of the author's boxes above.

A ROUTER AND SLOT CUTTER substitute for a plate joiner. A steady hand and a keen eye (protected by safety glasses) will yield a strong, quick spline joint.

or join rail and stile for a frame-and-panel or glazed door, spline joints are useful.

The spline joint is easier than doweling and stronger, too. Locating the splines is easy because the critical dimension is controlled by the depth setting of the router (see the right photo on the facing page). Just be sure to index from the same face, and whatever you're joining with splines will be in the same plane. Since I already have several routers, it's a lot cheaper to use a slotting cutter and splines than to buy a dedicated plate joiner, which makes a similar, though less adaptable, joint. Also, I use mostly scrap plywood for my splines, so there's less chance of swelling or having the spline telegraph through to the surface than with conventional compressed birch biscuits.

The Right Equipment: A Good Slotting Cutter

Other than a router, the only item you need for spline joinery is a slotting cutter, a generally available router bit. These come in many diameters and slot widths, but choosing the right one needn't be confusing. There are two general rules. First, select the largest shank size your router will accommodate—usually ½ in. And second, go with the smallest diameter cutter you can find because a ¼-in. shank and a 1¾-in. cutter make a weak and dangerous combination. I have a couple of bent shanks in my collection, as well as ruined router bases, due to the mass of the cutter being too great for the shank.

My favorite bit has a ½-in. shank, 1⅝₆-in. cutter and a ¾-in. pilot bearing. That means there's just over ¼ in. of cutter in the wood, and the ½-in. shank can handle that easily. Also, the depth of cut, which is actually ⅝₂ in., means that your spline is more than ½ in. wide (⅝₂ plus ⅝₂ is ⅝₆), making for a strong joint.

Cutter widths vary from ⅟₃₂ in. up to ½ in. or so. Most of my structural joints are made with a ¼-in. cutter. When joining a frame that is also taking a ¼-in. plywood panel, it's necessary to use two ⅝₂-in. cutters with a thin washer between them to make a slot that hugs the undersize plywood.

Making Splines

Splines can be made from a variety of materials, including medium-density fiberboard (MDF), plywood, and solid wood. My favorite is planed-to-order Baltic birch. I use it all the time for drawers, so there's

SLOTS FOR FRAME JOINERY AND PANEL can be routed simultaneously with a pair of ³⁄₃₂-in. cutters separated by a thin washer. The result is a strong frame and a snugly fitting panel.

USE SOLID END PIECES with plywood splines to get maximum strength without sacrificing looks or speed.

plenty of scrap. When joining solid boards edge to edge, as for tabletops, I rip thin sections of spline material. When I'm using biscuit-shaped splines to join rails and stiles to make frames, I bandsaw the splines to rough size and then shape them on either my stationary belt sander or a sanding drum on my drill press (see the photo on p. 43).

If you use solid wood for splines, make sure the grain runs across the joint, rather than parallel to it, for maximum strength and to allow for seasonal wood movement. Frequently, I'll use plywood splines for all but the ends of a long joint, particularly large panel glue-ups, and just use small bits of solid wood at the ends where they'll show. This makes for a strong joint that looks nice and works well for tabletops and box lids (see the left photo on p. 42 and the photo above right).

Frame Joinery, Panel Alignment, and Decorative Edging

I've used slotting cutters for many purposes other than what they were intended for, including rabbeting all around the top edge

of a tabletop to inlay a strip of contrasting wood. The most common uses of the slotting cutter in my shop, however, are to join frames and to align and strengthen panels I'm gluing edge to edge.

When I'm joining a frame that takes a flat plywood panel, I make the panel and spline the same thickness and rout both the panel groove and the recess for the spline simultaneously. To do this, I stop just shy of the ends of the stiles and rout right around the ends of the rails, stopping shy of the outside edge (see the photo above left).

For glazed cabinet doors, I want to be able to remove the glass if it ever breaks, so I use the router and slotting cutter just as I would a plate joiner: I make blind slots in the ends of the rails and the top inside edges of the stiles (see the photos on the facing page). Then I come back later, adjust the router's depth of cut for a rabbet rather than a groove and create a recess for the glass. The corners will be round, but most glass shops will be glad to radius the corners of a sheet of glass for you.

STEVEN COOK is a professional woodworker and musical-instrument restorer in Edmonds, Washington.

A SLOT CUTTER MAKES A BLIND SPLINE RECESS in the end of the rail. The author makes the cut freehand, using a pencil line to set the limit of the spline groove.

MATING SLOTS ARE CUT IN THE STILES. With the router and slot cutter at the same setting, the author makes the stile slot. The depth setting of the router keeps everything in line as long as all cuts are from the same side of the frame.

PLYWOOD MAKES A BISCUIT-STYLE SPLINE. A piece of plywood sanded to shape fits snugly in the finished slot. The author will reset the depth of cut for a rabbet to create the recess for the glass.

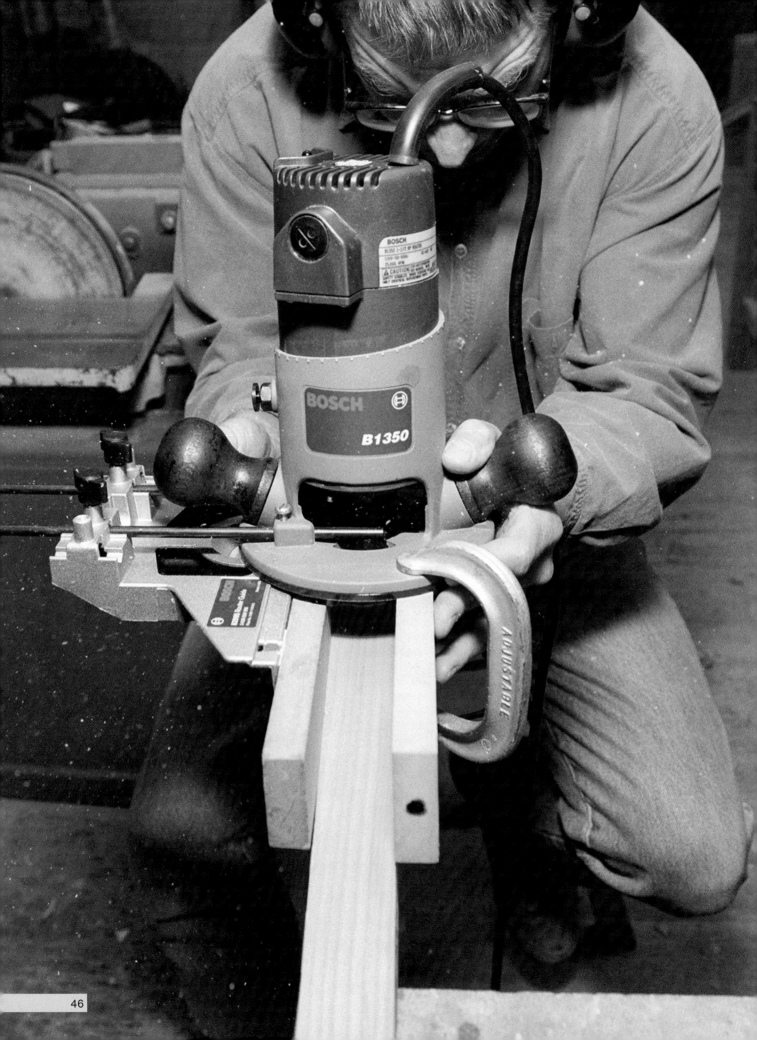

Mortising with a Router

I cut my first set of mortises by hand. It was a fabulous learning experience. I found that chopping through red oak was like digging postholes in dry clay. I had to resharpen my chisel after each mortise, but I learned. I also bought a router.

A router is the quickest and most accurate tool for cutting mortises. Its versatility and speed is unmatched, and it can be used in a variety of setups, both upright and upside down in a router table. In minutes, a router cuts mortises that would take hours by hand. And you can reproduce your results with a minimum of hassle or setup time. When I have mortises to cut these days, the router is my first choice. Either a fixed-base or a plunge router can produce excellent results.

Choosing the Right Bit

There are a variety of bit sizes and types that can be used for mortising. Two shank sizes are commonly available: ¼ in. and ½ in. Either will work, but bits with ½-in. shanks flex less under load, give a better cut, and are less likely to break.

I don't bother with high-speed steel (HSS) bits because they need to be sharpened too often. Carbide-tipped bits cost two to three times more but they last much longer. Solid-carbide bits are great, too, but they're even more expensive.

Straight bits come in two flavors: single flute for quick removal of material and double flute for a smooth finish. Because you'll find double-fluted bits in most tool catalogs, you'll get more size options.

The flutes of a spiral bit twist around the shank. This gives a shearing cut that is even smoother than one from a double-fluted straight bit. Spiral bits are available both in solid carbide and carbide-tipped steel. They spiral up or down.

BY GARY ROGOWSKI

TWO FENCES KEEP A ROUTER IN LINE. When routing to full depth with a fixed-base router, you want to make sure it doesn't veer out of the mortise.

MORTISING WITH A FIXED-BASE ROUTER

You will get a cleaner mortise by setting the bit to full depth right from the start. Cut the mortise in several passes with the router tipped at an angle.

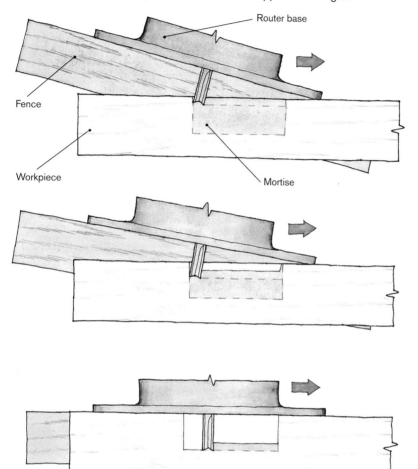

Router base

Fence

Workpiece

Mortise

First Pass

The first pass, with the router held at an angle, should remove about ⅛ in. to ¼ in. of material.

Second Pass

The angle of the router is lowered for the second pass, but bit depth remains the same. This and each successive pass removes from ⅛ in. to ¼ in.

Last Pass

The last pass is made with the router flat against the workpiece and the bit straight up and down.

An up-cut spiral bit cuts quickly while pulling most of the chips out of the mortise. However, it also will tend to pull the workpiece up if it's not securely fastened. The up-cut spiral also can leave a slightly ragged edge at the top of the mortise where wood fibers are unsupported. Because the edges of a mortise are usually covered by the shoulders of a tenon, this kind of tearout generally isn't a problem.

A down-cut spiral bit pushes the work and the chips down. The result is a cleaner mortise but one that can become clogged with debris.

I have used mostly double-fluted straight bits and a carbide-tipped up-cut spiral bit. Recently, though, I bought a solid-carbide up-cut spiral, which cuts even better.

Using a Fixed-Base Router

If the only router you have is a fixed-base router, you're not out of luck. It will just take a little more attention to detail and skill to get good mortises than it would with a plunge router.

A straight fence attached to the router is essential for accurately guiding the cut. Adding a long wooden auxiliary fence to

MULTIPLE DEPTH SETTINGS CREATE STEPS.
To adjust the bit height on most fixed-base routers, you have to twist the motor in its base. This often results in stepped, sloppy sidewalls.

your router's stock fence will give the router more stability. A second fence, clamped to the router base and on the other side of the workpiece, is a good idea, too (see the photo on p. 47). This fixes the position of the router laterally, so it can't accidentally slip to one side or the other during the cut. Combined with end stops, a double

fence will virtually ensure accurately located mortises. The only thing left to set is the depth, and here you have a choice of methods.

Multiple Depth Settings One way of mortising with a fixed-base router is to take just a little bite with each pass, gradually lowering the bit until you're at full depth. The biggest drawback with this approach is that it's hard to get a smooth-walled mortise. The reason is that the motor and, consequently, the bit may not stay centered in the base as you adjust the depth of cut.

With most routers, adjusting the bit height requires that you turn the motor in the base housing. When you do, the bit moves in relation to the fence, only slightly, but enough to give the walls of the mortise a stepped, rough surface (see the photo above). Exceptions are the DeWalt, Black & Decker, and Elu routers, which employ a rack-and-pinion adjustment system that keeps the collet and bit centered at a fixed distance from the fence.

WITH HARDBOARD SHIMS, YOU SET THE BIT JUST ONCE.
By removing one shim after each pass, you can take safe, manageable bites without having to change the router's depth setting. Increments of either ¼ in. or ⅛ in. are possible.

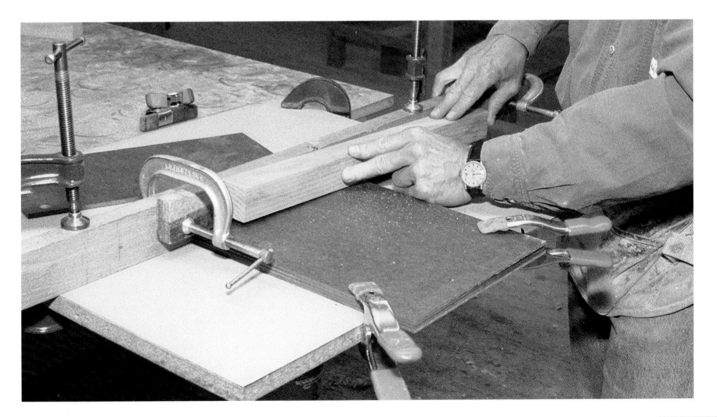

LAYOUT LINES ARE MUCH EASIER TO SEE WHEN
THEY'RE NOT HIDDEN. **The pencil marks show
where the router base should stop, and the tick
marks indicate that you're getting close.**

STOPS ARE FOOLPROOF. **Clamp or screw stops in place to limit the travel of the router,
front and back. You won't have to worry about trying to see layout marks when the
chips are flying.**

One Depth Setting One way around this
stepping problem is to set the bit at full
depth right from the start. To mortise, you
just move the router at an angle to the
workpiece so you introduce a little more of
the bit to the wood with each pass (see the
drawing on p. 48 and the photo on p. 47).
The router is tilted, resting on one edge of
its base, until the final pass is made. An extra-
wide auxiliary fence is advisable, and a second fence clamped to the router base on
the other side of the workpiece is essential.

Router-Table Mortises

Why would anyone want to cut mortises on
a router table? Well, for narrower stock, a
router table provides plenty of support.
When routing narrow pieces from above,
a handheld router can become tippy and
unstable. The edge of a door stile, for example, just doesn't offer very much support for
a router base. With a router table, you have
both the table and the fence against which
to register the workpiece, and only you have
the weight of the workpiece to control. For

small table legs or cabinet doors, mortising
on the router table is worth trying.

When mortising on a router table, use
the fence to position the mortise from side
to side and stops to establish the ends of the
mortise. As you face the table, the work
should move from right to left. This feed
direction will help keep the work tight
against the fence. Start with the workpiece
against the right-hand stop, and lower the
work into the bit. Because most bits don't
cut in the center, it helps to lower and
simultaneously move the work along just a
little to avoid burning. Move the workpiece
from right to left across the bit until it hits
the other stop.

If you're using a plunge router, you can
set the turret stops for incremental cuts,
make three passes and finish up at full
depth. But if you're using a fixed-base
router, you'll have a problem getting a
smooth-walled mortise if you adjust the
bit height between passes—just as you
would when using the router upright.

ONE FIXTURE CUTS MANY
MORTISES. **This simple
U-shaped box is one of the
most versatile mortising
fixtures you can build.**

My solution to this problem is to use shims made from ¼-in. hardboard, like Masonite, notched around the bit, to elevate the workpiece above the table (see the bottom photo on p. 49). In this way, I can set the bit at full height and just remove a shim after each cut, gradually working down until the workpiece is on the table and the last cut is made.

Mortising with a Plunge Router

The best tool for mortising is the plunge router used on top of the work. This is the job it was designed for. There are many different kinds of fixtures that can be used with the plunge router. Two that I use frequently, a U-shaped box and a template with a fence, are discussed below.

There are several schools of thought as to how to plunge the bit into the work. One method is to plunge a full-depth hole at each end of the mortise and then make a series of cleanup passes between those two holes. The drawback to this method is that you may get some burning as you plunge to full depth because most bits don't have center-cutting capability.

Alternately, you can make a series of successively deeper, full-length passes, always moving left to right with the bit lowered and locked in place each time. For me, making full passes without locking the plunge mechanism on each pass works best.

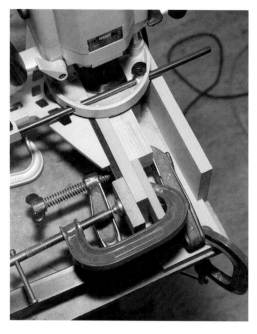

MEASURE ONCE, AND CLAMP A STOP IN PLACE. The less measuring you have to do, the fewer errors you're likely to make. The stop on the inside of the fixture positions the workpiece. The one on the outside is a fence stop, which establishes one end of the mortise.

U-Shaped Mortising Fixture

This router fixture is simple to make and incredibly versatile. It can be made to accommodate a wide range of work and takes only a few minutes to set up for a mortising operation.

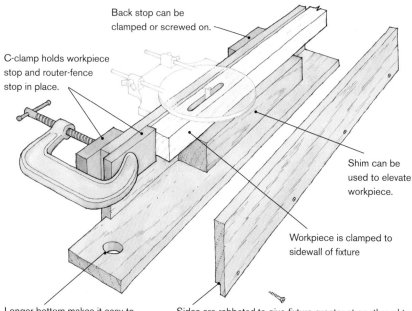

Back stop can be clamped or screwed on.

C-clamp holds workpiece stop and router-fence stop in place.

Shim can be used to elevate workpiece.

Workpiece is clamped to sidewall of fixture

Longer bottom makes it easy to clamp fixture to workbench. Hole near end is used to hang fixture.

Sides are rabbeted to give fixture greater strength and to ease assembly. The sides are glued and screwed to the bottom.

I keep the router moving. Try each of these methods to see which one works best for you.

Using a Stock Router Fence The simplest method for mortising with a plunge router is to mark the mortise ends on the workpiece and to set the last turret stop for the full depth of the mortise.

To adjust the bit's position, place the router on a marked-out workpiece, and lower the bit so it's just touching the surface of the work. Rotate the bit so its cutting edges are in line with the width of the mortise. Adjust the fence so it's flush against the side of the workpiece and the edges of the bit are within the layout lines. Then clamp the workpiece firmly to the bench, and rout away. Keep in mind, though, that the router will be tippy on narrow stock.

You can try to bring the bit just up to the end marks of the mortise with each pass, but it can be difficult to see them with all those chips flying around. Another way to accomplish this is to line up the edges of the bit at both ends of the mortise and make a pencil mark at the outside edge of the router base (see the left photo on p. 50). These marks are a lot easier to see than layout lines at the ends of the mortise.

If you're concerned about cutting beyond the layout lines, just clamp on stops to limit router travel. It only takes a second. Clamp the stops directly onto the workpiece once you've determined the length of the mortise (see the right photo on p. 50).

Mortising with the U-Shaped Box One of the most versatile router-mortising fixtures that I've come across is a simple U-shaped box (see the drawing at left). I first saw one of these boxes in a magazine article by Tage Frid. Since then, I've made a number of them dedicated to particular pieces of furniture.

But having one fixture that handles a variety of different-size parts is really useful, too. The one in the photo on p. 51 is

A TEMPLATE GUIDE SCREWS TO THE ROUTER BASE. **The guide's rub collar follows a slot cut in the template.**

STOPS ARE BUILT IN. **A template prevents side-to-side movement of the bit and automatically sets the length of the mortise.**

USING A TEMPLATE AND A GUIDE TO MORTISE

Routing mortises with a hardboard template and router-template guide is quick and virtually foolproof. The size of the slot in the hardboard determines the size of the mortise. The template is clamped to the workpiece, and the assembly is then clamped to the bench.

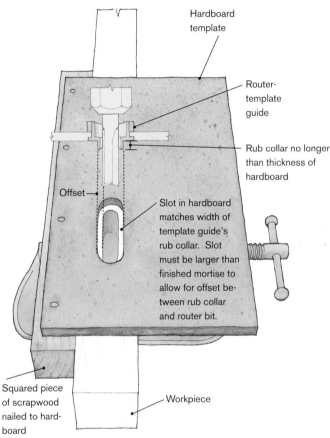

Hardboard template

Router-template guide

Rub collar no longer than thickness of hardboard

Offset

Slot in hardboard matches width of template guide's rub collar. Slot must be larger than finished mortise to allow for offset between rub collar and router bit.

Squared piece of scrapwood nailed to hardboard

Workpiece

made of ¾-in.-thick medium-density fiberboard (MDF). Its sides are rabbeted for the bottom (this helps align it during assembly). I also made the bottom longer than the side walls so I could clamp it down easily to any work surface.

The best way to deal with multiple identical mortises is to clamp an end stop to the side wall of the fixture (see the photo on the facing page). This way, each new piece will automatically be fixed in the right spot. Stops to index the mortise length also can be clamped onto the fixture. I prefer clamping these on rather than

using an adjustable stop—I don't want to risk the stop being nudged out of place.

When placing the workpiece in the fixture, always make sure the piece is sitting flat on the fixture bottom and tight to the inside wall and end stop. Clamp the workpiece securely. Spacers can be used underneath pieces to bring them higher in the fixture or to push a piece away from the sidewall. Make sure the spacers are milled flat and support the workpiece well. Be sure that the clamps holding the work don't get in the way of the router.

To improve stability, attach a wooden auxiliary fence to the one that comes with the plunge router. Then position the bit in the right spot. Remember to hold the fence tightly to the wall and to move the router so the fence will be drawn up against the wall of the fixture by the rotation of the bit.

Dedicated mortising fixtures are extremely useful when you plan to reproduce a number of cuts on a regular basis. I made an angled fixture to cut the mortises for a stool I build at least once a year. The end stop locates each leg in the proper spot.

A spacer block positioned against the stop locates the second set of mortises in the legs. Stops screwed to the outside of the fixture wall limit the length of travel of the fence and, therefore, produce mortises that are the correct length.

Templates and Template Guides A template guide is a round metal plate with a thin-walled rub collar that extends out from its base (see the top photo on page 53). The guide is screwed to the router base, and a router bit fits through it without touching the inside wall of the collar. The outer wall of the rub collar is guided by a straight edge or template as the router cuts (see the bottom photo on page 53).

Templates that are made of hardboard, plywood, or MDF include a slot to guide the rub collar as it makes the cut. The template is clamped to a workpiece with its slot centered over the mortise. I make up a template for a mortise when I'm doing a job I expect to repeat.

To make a template, nail a piece of $\frac{1}{4}$-in. hardboard about 5 in. wide and 10 in. long to a piece of wood approximately 2 in. sq. and a little longer than the hardboard (see the drawing on page 53).

The wood block is the fence, and the hardboard gets a slot cut in it that is exactly the width of the rub collar. Cut the slot in the template on the router table. To be sure the slot is parallel with the fence—which

ensures that the mortise is square to the stock you're routing—tack the hardboard back a little bit from the edge.

Set up the router table with a straight bit that matches the outside dimension of the rub collar. The template slot is pencil-marked on the hardboard. The diameter of the template guide is greater than that of the bit you'll use when mortising. So you'll need to add the distance from the outside of the rub collar to the edge of the router bit to each end of the slot in the template (see the drawing on page 53). Typically, this offset is between $\frac{1}{16}$ in. and $\frac{1}{8}$ in.

Before cutting the slot in the hardboard template, take a minute to determine the setback from the edge of the workpiece to the edge of the mortise. Then set the router-table fence accordingly. I like to double-check that the fence is in the right spot. So I make a nibble cut at the end of the template, and then measure the distance from that point to the fence. This method ensures that you get the correct distance. Once you have it, plunge the template down onto the bit as close to the center of the slot as possible, and then slide the template back and forth just up to the pencil marks at each end.

Templates like these are versatile. For example, a template made to cut a mortise $\frac{3}{4}$ in. from the edge of a table leg also could be used to cut the same sized mortise $\frac{1}{2}$ in. from the edge. How? Simply by inserting a $\frac{1}{4}$-in. shim between the template fence and the workpiece.

Once you have made the template and clamped it to the workpiece, position the plunge router with the template guide on the work. Set the bit depth, taking into account the thickness of the template. An up-cut spiral bit will pull most of the debris out of the mortise as the cut is made.

GARY ROGOWSKI designs and builds furniture in Portland, Oregon. He is a contributing editor to *Fine Woodworking.*

Floating-Tenon Joinery

BY LON SCHLEINING

Mortise-and-tenon joints are the building blocks of furniture making. Once you have a simple and reliable system for making them, joinery on tables, chairs, and case goods is straight-forward, fast, and consistent, even when there are compound angles.

The distance between the shoulders is critical in the case of something like a table apron or a chair stretcher. One day I had cut a big pile of pieces to length, only to discover that I'd made one teensy mistake: I had forgotten to allow for the extra tenon length on both ends of the pieces. That's when I began to rethink my resistance to using floating tenons. With floating tenons, you simply cut the piece to exact length, and it's done. The shoulders fit perfectly, eliminating one of the most frustrating parts of mortise-and-tenon joinery.

In a joint-strength test in 2002 conducted by the *Fine Woodworking* staff, floating tenons compared favorably to traditional mortise-and-tenon joints, putting to rest common doubts about their performance.

A floating tenon is a separate piece inserted into matching mortises in two mating pieces. Similar to biscuit joinery, you cut a mortise into each of the pieces

THIS SIMPLE JIG works with a plunge router to make quick, strong joints.

to be joined—leg and apron, rail and stile. Then you mill tenon stock to fit the mortises, cut it to length and assemble the joint.

Make a Router Jig for This Joinery

There are many ways to cut mortises, but this router jig is my favorite for floating-tenon joinery. It will create precise, matching mortises in both the sides and ends of workpieces, and it's easy to make using birch plywood, screws, glue, and a few hardwood blocks.

This jig shown will cut a mortise 1 in. from the clamping fence, meaning the mortise will be centered in 2-in.-thick stock. This large capacity adapts well to a variety of projects and joints. If your workpieces are thinner, for example, or you'd like a reveal with a thinner member centered on a leg, post or stile, or even if you want an angled mortise, the jig is easily adapted with a few shims.

You can change the starting dimensions of this jig to suit the mortise you cut most often, or you can build several variations, as I have, each with a specific purpose.

Build It Accurately or Suffer Later

This jig is designed to last—turning out lots of accurate joints. So take your time.

Set-Up Blocks Are the Key to Making an Accurate Jig

1 ATTACH THE GUIDE BLOCKS

This mortising jig relies on guide blocks to limit the travel of the router. Make a set-up block, which represents the overall travel of the router base, for gluing the guide blocks to the jig base squarely and accurately.

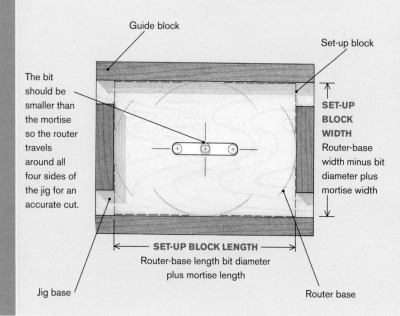

Guide block

Set-up block

The bit should be smaller than the mortise so the router travels around all four sides of the jig for an accurate cut.

SET-UP BLOCK WIDTH
Router-base width minus bit diameter plus mortise width

SET-UP BLOCK LENGTH
Router-base length bit diameter plus mortise length

Jig base

Router base

THE GUIDE BLOCKS ARE GLUED TO THE BASE OF THE JIG. Clamp the guide blocks both to the set-up block (center) and to the top face of the jig. Thin packing tape on the set-up block makes it easier to remove after glue-up.

The first step in the assembly is to glue four blocks to the base of the jig. These blocks guide the router base. *Note*: Even round-based routers tend to be off center slightly, so it's important to keep the router facing in a single direction when you use the jig.

The easiest way to keep the guide blocks square and parallel during glue-up is to cut a set-up block the size of the area inside the guide blocks. Clamp the guide blocks to the set-up block before clamping and gluing them to the plywood base.

Once the glue cures, remove the set-up block and use a router and ⅜-in. bit to plunge-cut the mortise slot into the base.

Next, draw the centerlines on both the top and bottom of the base. These lines must be drawn carefully because they'll be the reference lines for every cut you make.

Attaching the clamping fence is the other important part of the assembly. If the fence is misaligned or out of parallel even slightly, the mortise-and-tenon joint won't come together as it should.

To lock in the distance between the fence and the mortise's centerline, make another set-up block (1 in. thick for this jig). Clamp the block to the base, aligning its edge with the mortise slot's center, then clamp the fence to the block and the base and drill the pilot and clearance holes for

2 ATTACH THE FENCE TO THE BOTTOM

A fence on the underside of the base locates the workpiece. Use another set-up block to locate the fence accurately.

FIRST, ROUT THE MORTISE SLOT IN THE BASE. The blue tape on the handle and the jig records the correct orientation of the router.

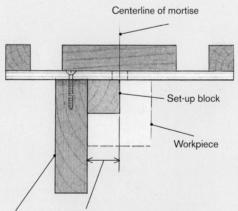

Centerline of mortise

Set-up block

Workpiece

Fence

Make a set-up block equal to the distance between the edge of the workpiece and the center of the mortise. Use the block to attach the fence.

CAREFULLY MARK THE CENTERLINE OF THE MORTISE AND CLAMP THE SET-UP BLOCK IN PLACE. Clamp the fence to both the block and the jig when gluing it down. Add screws from above the jig base.

Using the Jig

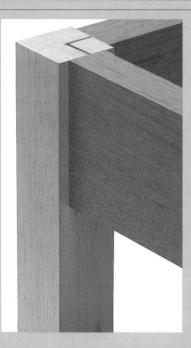

The author sized this jig to handle the thickest workpiece—a 2-in.-thick table leg—that he commonly mortises. To mortise the thinner rail, add a shim to the jig.

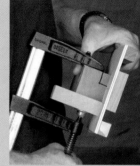

LAY OUT THE WORKPIECES CAREFULLY. Mark the outer reference faces of each piece, and transfer the centerline of the desired mortise from one piece to the other.

ALIGN THE CENTERLINE WITH CENTER MARKS ON THE JIG. Then clamp the workpiece in place. The mark on the end grain (right) signifies the mortised sides of this table leg.

ADD A SHIM FOR THINNER STOCK

Centerline of mortise

Shim

Workpiece

Fence

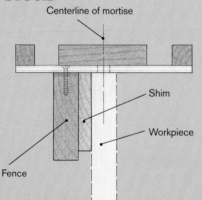

3 ROUT IN A FEW PASSES FOR A CLEAN MORTISE. Clamp the jig's fence sideways in a vise to secure the setup. The bit is smaller than the mortise, so move the router clockwise around the jig for an accurate cut.

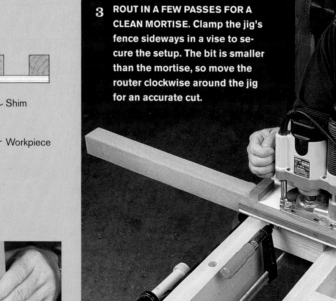

THINNER WORKPIECES ARE NO PROBLEM. This shim is sized to center the mortise in the rails, creating a ½-in. reveal between the rail and the leg.

PLANE THE TENON STOCK TO THICKNESS. **Test often for fit, then round the edges with a roundover bit on the router table.**

the screws. Use 1½-in.-long screws, countersinking them so that they sit flush in the base.

Remove the fence temporarily and spread on some glue. Then clamp up everything again and tighten the screws.

Cut Matching Mortises

As always for mortise-and-tenon joinery, start by marking the reference faces of your workpieces—for example, the front side of stiles and the corresponding faces of rails. Whether the mortises are in a table, a chair, or a frame, corresponding faces should go against the clamping fence of the jig to make sure they line up correctly later.

To lay out the mortises themselves, all you need to do is mark their centerlines.

Rout in Several Passes It's a good idea to cut the 1-in.-deep mortises in at least two or three passes. It puts too much strain on the bit and the machine to cut it all at once. If your router has a stepped depth adjustment, now's the time to use it.

Because this jig guides the base of the router, accumulated chips and dust can change the path of the bit. If your router doesn't have dust collection built in, cut the

AS ALWAYS, DRY-FIT BEFORE GLUE-UP. **The tenons should fit snugly but not require excessive force to fit.**

mortise, vacuum out the jig and the mortise, then take a final pass.

Use a straight bit with a ½-in. shank, designed for plunge cutting, with a cutting diameter slightly smaller than the desired mortise. By making a pass around all four sides of the jig, you can better control the width of the mortise. Otherwise, the guide blocks would have to fit the router base exactly with absolutely no slop, a notion I find unrealistic.

A Word of Caution

The mortise routed into the end grain may come out at a slightly different width than the one made in the face grain. If you find a difference, add a layer or two of masking tape to the jig's guide blocks to cut one or the other.

Angled Joinery Made Easy

Cut the rail at the desired angle where it meets the post. When using the router jig to cut the mortise in the rail, just add an angled shim. Add an identical shim on the other side of the fence to keep the clamping force square. The post is mortised without angled shims.

Make Tenon Stock to Fit

It's straightforward to mill tenon stock once you've established the size of the mortises. First, use the same material that the mortised workpieces are made of, with the grain running the same direction as it does in the rail. This will help at least one side of the floating-tenon joint expand and contract similarly. Cut the tenon board long enough to cut all of the tenons with plenty left over to trim planer snipe from the ends.

Rip the tenon board $\frac{1}{16}$ in. smaller than the length of the mortise. This does three important things: It allows a little leeway for aligning the rails and stiles during glue-up, gives excess glue a way to escape, and allows for the uneven expansion and contraction of the tenon and the mortise in the leg or stile.

Using a planer, reduce the board to the thickness of the mortise. When you get close, test-fit the corner of the tenon board in the mortise, then crank down the planer a little at a time until you get a snug fit. Beware of the snipe that most planers leave on the ends of boards. Chop off this area before each test fitting.

Next, using a $\frac{3}{16}$-in. roundover bit, round each edge of the tenon stock. This radius will match the one left by the $\frac{3}{8}$-in.-dia. router bit used to cut the mortises. The tenon should fit into the mortises snugly—without having to be forced in and without falling out when held upside down. Last, cut the tenons to length, about $\frac{1}{8}$ in. shy of the combined depths of the mortises: for example, $1\frac{7}{8}$ in. long for two 1-in.-deep mortises. Test the fit, then glue up the joint. That's all there is to it.

Jig Can Be Adapted to Many Mortises

If your workpieces are narrower than the ones this jig is set up for—maybe you're joining $\frac{3}{4}$-in.-thick rails and stiles—simply add a shim between the workpiece and the clamping fence (see the sidebar on p. 58).

Another frequent adaptation you'll make is to change the mortise length. Let's say the rail on a chair is 2 in. tall; obviously, the $2\frac{3}{4}$-in.-tall mortise would be too large. But adding blocks to the guides at each end of the jig shorten the mortise. You should adjust both ends equally, because the jig uses centerlines to position the workpiece.

If the mortise is too short for your project—let's say a table with a tall apron or a breadboard end—you can slide the jig along the workpiece to cut two or more mortises in a row. This jig even makes angled joints easier (see the photos in the sidebar above).

Once you get the hang of it, this is the sort of jig you'll use all the time.

LON SCHLEINING, a contributing editor to *Fine Woodworking*, teaches about woodworking throughout the country.

Router Fixture Takes on Angled Tenons

We live in a turn-of-the-century Arts-and-Crafts house, so it seemed quite natural to furnish it with pieces from that era. My wife bought a pair of Mission armchairs a couple of years ago to go with a 9-ft.-long cherry table I'd built for our dining room. Six months later, she bought two side chairs. It would be a while before we could afford a full set. Within earshot of my wife, I heard myself say, "How hard could it be to make these?"

"Oh, could you?" she asked.

"Sure," I said. The chairs looked straightforward enough, just a cube with a back. Upon closer examination, I realized that the seat was slightly higher and wider in the front than in the back. For the first

BY EDWARD KOIZUMI

THIS VERSATILE DEVICE ensures tight joints every time.

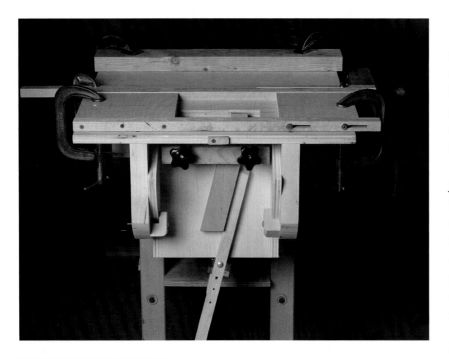

time, I was faced with compound-angled joinery. I thought about dowels, biscuits and loose tenons, so I could keep the joinery simple, but I wasn't confident in the strength or longevity of these methods.

I wanted good, old-fashioned, dependable mortise-and-tenon joints. After some thought, I decided an adjustable router fixture would be the simplest solution that would let me make tenons of widely varying sizes and angles (see the photo on p. 61).

The fixture I came up with is as easy to set up as a tablesaw. In fact, there are some similarities (see the drawing on the facing page). The workpiece is held below a tabletop in a trunnion-type assembly that adjusts the tilt angle (see the photo above). For compound angles, a miter bar rotates the workpiece in the other plane. The fixture can handle stock up to 2 in. thick and 5 in. wide (at 0°-0°) and angles up to 25° in one plane and 20° in the other. This is sufficient for chairs, which seldom have angles more than 5°.

To guide the router during the cut, I clamp a guide frame to the fixture over the window in the tabletop (more on positioning it later). And I plunge rout around the tenon on the end of the workpiece. The

guide frame determines the tenon's width and length, as well as whether the ends will be square or round (see the left photo on p. 67). I made two frames, both adjustable, one for round-cornered tenons, the other for square tenons.

The fixture and guide frames took me just over a day to make, once I'd figured out the design. Then I spent about an hour aligning the fixture and making test tenons in preparation for routing the tenons on the chair parts. The fixture worked just as planned and allowed this relatively inexperienced woodworker to produce eight chairs that match the originals perfectly.

Making the Fixture and Guide Frames

The fixture is simple to build. It consists of only two main parts, the trunnion assembly and the tabletop. The trunnion assembly (see the drawing on the facing page) is essentially a pair of arcs nestled between two pivot supports. Between the two arcs is a work platen, or surface, against which I clamp the component to be tenoned. There are other parts, but basically, the fixture is just a table to slide the router on and a movable platen to mount the workpiece on.

Building the Fixture I built the fixture from the inside out, beginning with the work platen (see the drawing on the facing page). Because I didn't have any means of boring a 10-in.-long hole for the threaded rod on which the arcs pivot, I dadoed a slot in the platen and then glued in a filler strip. Next I located, center punched, and drilled the holes for the T-nuts and retaining nuts that hold the clamping studs in place. Center punching ensures that the holes are exactly where they're supposed to be, which is important for a fixture that's going to be used over and over again. I center-punched the location for every hole in this fixture before drilling.

TENON-ROUTING FIXTURE FOR COMPOUND ANGLES

This fixture, adjustable in two planes, is designed to let you rout compound-angled tenons consistently and accurately. The tenons can be either squared or rounded, depending on which guide frame you use.

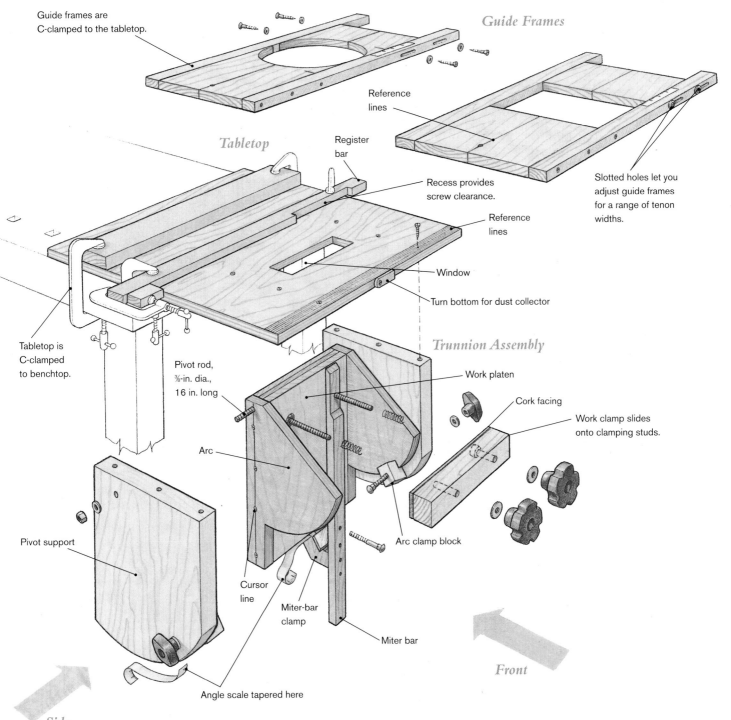

Guide Frames

Guide frames are C-clamped to the tabletop.

Reference lines

Slotted holes let you adjust guide frames for a range of tenon widths.

Tabletop

Register bar

Recess provides screw clearance.

Reference lines

Window

Turn bottom for dust collector

Tabletop is C-clamped to benchtop.

Pivot rod, ⅜-in. dia., 16 in. long

Trunnion Assembly

Work platen

Cork facing

Work clamp slides onto clamping studs.

Arc

Arc clamp block

Pivot support

Cursor line

Miter-bar clamp

Miter bar

Angle scale tapered here

Side

Front

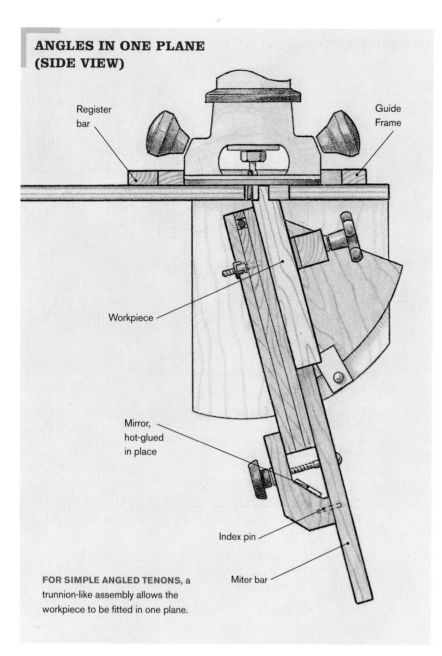

ANGLES IN ONE PLANE (SIDE VIEW)

Register bar

Guide Frame

Workpiece

Mirror, hot-glued in place

Index pin

Miter bar

FOR SIMPLE ANGLED TENONS, a trunnion-like assembly allows the workpiece to be fitted in one plane.

Before attaching the clamping studs to the work platen, I made the arcs, which go on the sides of the work platen. I laid out the arcs (and the pivot supports) with a compass, bandsawed and sanded the arcs, and drilled a hole for the pivot rod through the pair. I glued and screwed the arcs to the platen. After giving the glue an hour or so to set, I tapped the T-nuts into the back of the work platen, screwed in the clamping studs, and twisted on retaining nuts, which I tightened with a socket and a pair of pliers.

I made the pivot supports next. Then I cut a piece of threaded rod 16 in. long and deburred its ends with a mill file. I slipped the threaded rod through the pivot supports, arcs, and work platen, capped it at both ends with a nut and washer, and made and attached the arc clamps (see the drawing at left).

Then came the tabletop. I cut it to size, cut a window in it and marked reference lines every ⅛ in. along the front edge for the first 2 in. With the tabletop upside down on a pair of sawhorses, I put the trunnion assembly upside down on the underside of the tabletop. Then I positioned the front of the pivot supports against the front edge of the tabletop and made sure the work platen was precisely parallel to the front edge and centered left to right. That done, I drilled and countersunk holes for connecting screws through the tabletop into the pivot supports. I glued and screwed the pivot supports to the tabletop.

Then it was time to make the miter bar, miter-bar clamp, and the work clamp (see the drawings at left and on the facing page). The mirror on the miter-bar clamp makes it easy to read the angle scale from above. I faced the work clamp with cork to prevent marring workpieces and counterbored it to take up the release springs. The release springs are a nice touch. They exert a slight outward pressure on the work clamp, causing it to move away from the platen when loosening the knobs to remove a workpiece.

The Guide Frames Now for the guide frames, which clamp to the tabletop and limit the travel of the router. I made the frames adjustable lengthwise to handle a variety of tenoning situations. But their width is fixed. To determine the width of the frames, I added together the desired tenon width, the diameter of the bit I was using, and the diameter of the router base. If your plunge router does not have a round base, you should either make one from acrylic or polycarbonate (you can cut it with a circle-cutting jig on a bandsaw) or buy an aftermarket version. I screwed the frame together in case I need to alter the opening later (for a new router bit, for example). I marked a centerline along the length of the frame on both ends.

Initial Alignment

Before I could use the fixture, I had to get everything in proper alignment and put some angle scales on it. I printed out some angle scales from my computer and taped them to my fixture with double-faced tape. But a protractor and bevel gauge also will work just fine to create angle scales for both the tilt angle and the miter angle.

To align the parts of the fixture, I flipped it upside down on the end of my bench and clamped it there. I used a framing square to set both the work platen and the miter bar at 90°, sticking the blade of the square up through the window of the tabletop and resting the tongue of the square flush against the inverted face of the tabletop. Then I stuck the angle scales on the two pivot supports and on the bottom of the work platen.

Routing Test Tenons

Next I routed test tenons with the fixture set at 0°-0°. I positioned the guide frame parallel to the front edge and centered on the window in the tabletop and clamped it to the fixture. I clamped a test piece the

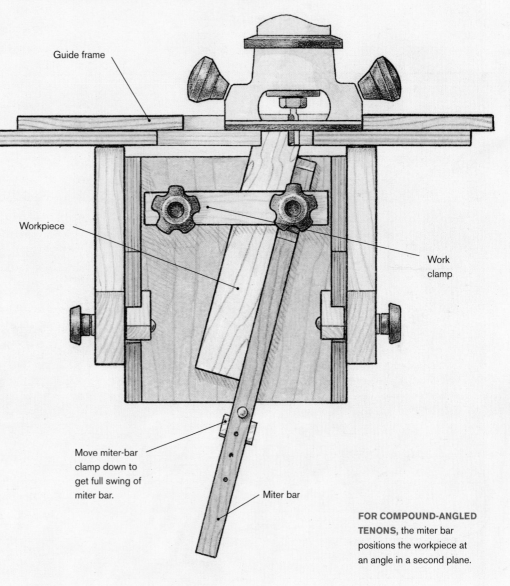

COMPOUND ANGLES (FRONT VIEW)

Guide frame

Workpiece

Work clamp

Move miter-bar clamp down to get full swing of miter bar.

Miter bar

FOR COMPOUND-ANGLED TENONS, the miter bar positions the workpiece at an angle in a second plane.

same thickness and width as the actual component in the fixture, with one end flush with the top surface of the tabletop. To do this, I brought the test piece up so that it just touched a flat bar lying across the window (see the top right photo on p. 66). I set my plunge router for the correct depth and routed the tenon clockwise to prevent tearout.

I made a test mortise using the same bit I planned to use for the mortises in the chair. The fit wasn't quite right. So I adjusted and shimmed the frame until the tenon fit

Setting Up for Angled Tenons

MARK OUT THE TENON ON A TEST PIECE. The test piece should be the same thickness and width as the actual components, but length isn't important.

MAKE THE WORKPIECE FLUSH WITH THE TABLETOP. The author uses a piece of milled steel, but the edge of a 6-in. ruler would work as well.

MAKE A PATTERN. An outline of the tenon traced on acetate helps align the guide frame for cutting any tenons of the same size.

perfectly. If you rout away too much material and end up with a sloppy tenon on your test piece, you can just lop off the end and start over.

Once I had a tenon that was dead-on, I made an acetate pattern that allowed me to position the guide frame accurately for all tenons of the same size, regardless of the angle. I cut a heavy sheet of acetate (available at most art-supply stores) so that it would just fit into the guide-frame opening. I marked a centerline along the length of the acetate that lines up with the centerline down both ends of the guide frames. I also indicated which end was up and where the acetate registered against the guide frame. Then I put the test piece with the perfectly fitted tenon back into the fixture, laid the acetate into the opening in the guide frame and traced around the perimeter of the tenon end using a fine-tip permanent marker.

Routing Angled Tenons

With the pattern, routing angled tenons is pretty straightforward. I crosscut the ends of all the pieces I was tenoning at the appropriate angles and marked out the first tenon of each type on two adjacent sides, taking the angles off a set of full-scale plans. Then I extended the lines up and across the end of the workpiece (see the top left photo).

Having set the fixture to the correct angles, I brought the workpiece flush with the tabletop using a flat piece of steel as a reference (see the top right photo). Then I clamped the workpiece in place. Finally, I set the acetate pattern in the guide-frame opening and positioned the guide frame so that the pattern and the marked tenon were perfectly aligned (see the bottom left photo). With the guide frame clamped in place, I removed the acetate and routed that tenon. All other identical tenons needed only to be flushed up and routed. After the first, it was quick work.

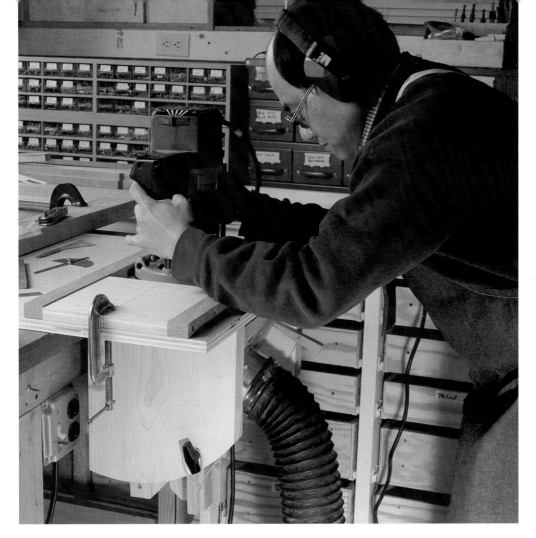

SET CORRECTLY, THE FIXTURE WILL YIELD TIGHT JOINTS, **whether the tenons are straight, angled or compound-angled. Here, the author tests the fit of a seat-rail tenon into a leg mortise.**

GUIDE FRAME DETERMINES THICKNESS AND WIDTH OF TENONS. **The author keeps the router's base against the inner edges of the guide frame and routs clockwise to prevent tearout. Guide frames can produce round-cornered or square-cornered tenons.**

There are pitfalls though. I found it important to chalk orientation marks on each workpiece. It can get confusing with two angles, each with two possible directions. And I had to be especially careful when routing the second end of a component. Make sure it's oriented correctly relative to the first. I messed up a couple of times and have learned to plan for mistakes by milling extra parts and test pieces. You might even end up with an extra chair.

To get flat surfaces on curved parts so I could clamp them in the fixture, I saved the complementary offcuts and taped them to the piece I was tenoning. Or I could have tenoned first and bandsawed the curves later.

For pieces with shoulders wider than the bit I'm using to remove waste, I clamp a straight piece of wood—a register bar—against the guide frame (a small pocket for

screw clearance may need to be made), as shown in the drawing on p. 63. That way I can rout most of the tenon, unclamp the guide frame, slide it forward (using the reference lines at the forward end of the tabletop to keep it parallel), clamp it down and then rout the remainder. I start the next piece in the same place and return the guide frame to the original position to finish the tenon.

EDWARD KOIZUMI is a professional model maker in Oak Park, Illinois.

End-Work Router Fixture

BY PATRICK WARNER

AN END-WORK PLATFORM HOLDS WORKPIECES VERTICALLY for cutting tenons or rounding the ends of frame members with a router. The slats attached to the bottom of the router keep it from tipping as the router passes over the window in the top of the fixture.

Routing or shaping the end of a board can be tricky. Even on a router table fitted with a fence, the small amount of surface area on the end of a board doesn't provide much stability when you run the piece vertically past the bit. And if the stock is long, the task is impossible because of the difficulty of handling a long piece on end. My router end-work fixture provides a safe and simple solution for routing the end of a board.

How the Fixture Works

Basically, this is the way the fixture works: A frame member or other workpiece is clamped to the fixture, which references it for the desired cut. The fixture's large platform top provides a stable support for the handheld router, and a window cutout in the platform allows access for the bit to shape the narrow end of the workpiece, as shown in the photo at left. The fixture features an indexing fence that's adjustable to facilitate angled tenons, such as those used to join seat rails to the rear leg of a chair.

The method of guiding the bit depends on the job. Some joints, such as stub tenons, can be done with a piloted rabbeting bit that rides the faces of the stock. An auxiliary router fence can be used to create more complicated tenons, sliding dovetails or other shapes on the end of stock, including roundovers or chamfers. The stock can be any shape—square, rectangular or even round, as shown in the top left photo on the following page.

Practically any bit normally used on the edge or face of a board can be used with this fixture. Because the router bit slices the wood fibers parallel to the grain when shaping the end of a board, the fibers are effortlessly peeled away rather than sheared, as is the case with cross-grain router cuts.

Building the Fixture

The parts for the fixture can be made from any hardwood (I used birch) or a good-grade of ¾-in. or 1-in. medium-density fiberboard (MDF). The fixture consists of a router platform with a rectangular window cutout for the router bit; a workpiece clamping board, joined at 90° to the platform with a tongue and groove and reinforced by two corner braces; and an adjustable indexing fence (see the drawing on p. 70).

After cutting the platform to size, I rout a ⅜-in.-wide by ³⁄₁₆-in.-deep groove the length of the bottom surface by running the router's accessory fence along the edge of the platform to ensure that the face of the clamping board will be parallel to the edge. I cut the window slightly undersized with a sabersaw and trim it to final size with a router and flush trimming bit following a template. A 3¾-in. by 6-in. window allows routing on stock up to 2 in. by 4 in. with bits up to 1½ in. dia. If larger stock or bigger cutters are used, make the window and/or platform larger.

After cutting the clamping board to size and rabbeting its top edges to form the tongue, I cut out a portion of the top edge for router bit clearance when the fixture is put to work. I rough out the cut with a sabersaw and trim it using one side of the same template I used for the platform window. The 1³⁄₁₆-in. by 6¼-in. cutout in the drawing allows for routing workpieces to a depth of about 1⅞ in. (if you take deeper cuts, make the cutout deeper, too). I band-saw the corner braces from 1⁵⁄₁₆-in.-thick pieces about 4¼ in. sq.

I use the tongue-and-groove joint to accurately register the clamping board to the platform, but I screw all the parts together instead of gluing them, so it's easier to disassemble and realign the parts later if necessary. To ensure that the screw holes in the platform align perfectly with those in the clamping board, I first drill four ¹³⁄₆₄-in.-dia. holes (for #10 flat-head screws) in the platform—

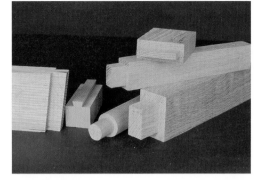

A VARIETY OF JOINTS CAN BE ROUTED with the end-work platform, including all kinds of square or angled tenons and sliding dovetails. Tenons can even be routed on the ends of round stock.

SHAPING TENONS WITH A PILOTED RABBET BIT is simple: The pilot bearing rides on the face of the workpiece as the short tenon is cut.

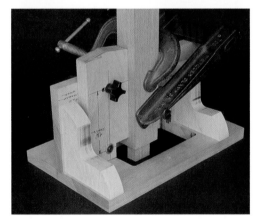

AFTER SETTING THE ADJUSTABLE INDEXING FENCE for shaping either a square or angled tenon, the fixture is held upside down on a flat surface, and the workpiece is clamped in place with its end flush with the top of the router platform. The fixture is then flipped over and clamped in a bench vise for routing.

two on either side of the window and centered on the groove. Then I use a ¹³⁄₆₄-in.-dia. transfer punch to mark the pattern for the pilot holes from the platform to the clamping board. I also use the same punch along with a countersink to perfectly prepare the holes for the heads of #10 flat-head screws. I use the same transfer and drilling process for drilling pilot holes in the corner braces.

Adjustable Fence Now I saw out the adjustable fence and cut out a 1-in.-sq. clearance notch from one corner, as shown in the drawing. I drill a ¼-in.-dia. hole, centered ¾ in. from the top end of the

Sources

Enco Manufacturing Co.
400 Nevada Pacific Hwy.
Fernley, NV 89408

W. L. Fuller, Inc.
P.O. Box 8767
Warwick, RI 02888
401-467-2900

fence, for a pivot pin. Then I fit my plunge router with a ¼-in.-dia. straight bit and a circle cutting jig for routing a curved slot in the fence. This curved slot, which is centered on the fence about 4⅛ in. from the pivot pin, allows the fence to be pivoted side to side and set either square to the platform or askew for angled tenons.

Next, I clamp the fence to the clamping board so that the fence's corner notch is aligned with the clamping board's clearance cutout, and its top edge is about ⅛ in. below the platform. Then I use a ¼-in.-dia. transfer punch to accurately mark the fence's pivot

hole and the center of the curved slot on the clamping board. These hole centers have to be precise, or the fence won't adjust easily. After drilling both holes with a ⁷⁄₃₂-in. drill bit, I thread the holes in the hardwood with a ¼–20 tap and install a 1¾-in.-long, ¼–20 machine screw for the pivot pin and a 1½-in.-long ¼–20 flat-head machine screw for the fence locking bolt. A threaded hand knob on the locking bolt makes fast fence adjustments without a wrench.

End Routing Stock

To use the fixture for routing basic tenons, first set the indexing fence 90° to the router platform. Set the fixture upside down on the bench, position the stock to be tenoned against the indexing fence with the stock's end flat on the bench, and secure it to the clamping board with C-clamps (see the bottom photo on p. 69). This indexes the workpiece square to, and flush with, the top surface of the platform. Flip the entire assembly over and clamp the workpiece in the bench vise so that the router platform is at a comfortable working height.

To eliminate any chance that the router will tip as it passes over the window in the fixture's platform, I screw a couple of ½-in.-thick strips of wood to the router base. If the desired cut can be made in a single pass, such as for a stub tenon, any standard router will do. Simply chuck up a piloted bit, set the cutting depth (which determines the tenon's length), and guide the bit around the stock (see the center photo on p. 69). Fit the router with an auxiliary guide that runs along the platform's edge when unpiloted cutters are used.

For deep cuts, a plunge router is my tool of choice. I set my plunge router's rotary depth stop to three different cutting heights and shape each tenon in three passes, resetting the stop to take a deeper cut each time.

PAT WARNER is a woodworker and college instructor who lives in Escondido, California.

ROUTER END-WORK FIXTURE

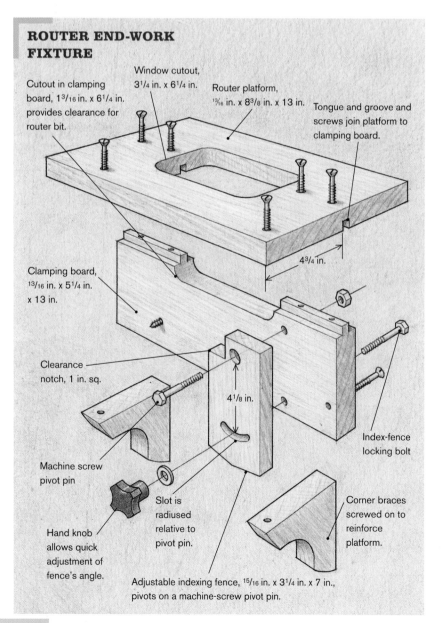

Cutout in clamping board, 1³⁄₁₆ in. x 6¼ in. provides clearance for router bit.

Window cutout, 3¼ in. x 6¼ in.

Router platform, 1³⁄₁₆ in. x 8⅜ in. x 13 in.

Tongue and groove and screws join platform to clamping board.

Clamping board, 1³⁄₁₆ in. x 5¼ in. x 13 in.

4¾ in.

Clearance notch, 1 in. sq.

4⅛ in.

Index-fence locking bolt

Machine screw pivot pin

Slot is radiused relative to pivot pin.

Corner braces screwed on to reinforce platform.

Hand knob allows quick adjustment of fence's angle.

Adjustable indexing fence, ¹⁵⁄₁₆ in. x 3¼ in. x 7 in., pivots on a machine-screw pivot pin.

Machinist's Transfer Punches Find a Niche in the Woodshop

Transfer punches are steel rods used to accurately mark the location of holes from an already drilled part to one that will be drilled to match. While they are tools from the machinist's chest, woodworkers can make good use of them as well. Typical jobs where transfer punches come in handy include drilling holes in a new router subbase using the old subbase as a pattern; locating and screwing a plinth or cornice to a carcase; and drilling pilot holes in jig parts that must fit accurately together. While any of these jobs can be accomplished with a scratch awl, using a transfer punch is much more accurate.

Sets of transfer punches are sold in either standard fractional or metric sizes as well as special drill letter and number sizes. I purchased my set, as shown in the top photo, for about $15 from Enco® Manufacturing Company, but they are also available at any good machinist supply house. Each punch is a few thousandths smaller in diameter than its corresponding drill size, so it's easy to slide in and out of an already drilled hole. The end of each rod is turned to a point so that it will put a dimple exactly in the center. To use a punch, first clamp the already drilled part in position over the part to be marked, insert the punch into the hole and lightly tap with a hammer. The slightly indented punch mark creates a starting dimple for the drill. Drill the new holes with a brad point bit, and you'll be amazed at the accuracy.

Other Uses

While punches excel at transferring hole positions, there are other uses for them in the woodshop. When drilling for flat-head wood screws, I often use an 82° countersink designed to be locked onto a drill bit with setscrews available from W. L. Fuller, Inc.. I've found that these countersinks work better when mounted on a transfer punch, as shown in the photo at right below. Using a transfer punch instead of a drill as a pilot has two advantages: The unfluted punch doesn't tear up the hole, and the countersink stays cooler because the smooth punch doesn't trap the chips produced by the countersink's cutters (as a drill bit does).

A transfer punch also can be used to center a previously drilled hole on the drill press either to counterbore it or to increase its depth or diameter. First tighten the appropriate-sized punch in the chuck, then lower it into the hole and lock the drill-press quill. Now you can clamp the part to the drill-press table, unlock the quill, insert the new bit and rebore as desired. A punch chucked in the drill press can also be used with a machinist's square to check the drill-press table for squareness to the bit. This same method also works to check square between a router's collet and a baseplate. A punch can be inserted into any hole, and its angle to the work surface can be checked with a machinist's square.

Finally, the rods can be used as form-sanding cauls for small coves. Because the punches come in almost any small diameter (less than 9/16 in.), the thickness of the abrasive can be compensated for, and a perfect fit obtained, by using a smaller punch than the desired cove. Also, each set of transfer punches comes in a holder, and the holes in these holders can be used as a drill gauge for those drill bits that have lost their identity.

A SET OF MACHINIST'S TRANSFER PUNCHES is a worthwhile investment for any woodshop. Not only do the precisely dimensioned punches provide a great way to transfer hole positions between parts, they can be used for other drill-press jobs, such as centering previously drilled holes.

A TRANSFER PUNCH CAN BE USED WITH A COUNTERSINK MOUNTED ON IT to cleanly and accurately prepare previously drilled holes for flat-head screws.

Turn a Router into a Joint-Making Machine

BY GUY PEREZ

I often turn to my router for joinery tasks. With a fence and straight bit, the router makes quick work of mortise-and-tenon joints. And for most projects, the consequent problem of either rounding the tenon or squaring the mortise is relatively minor. However, I recently made a crib with 44 slats that required 88 mortise-and-tenon joints. This daunting task prompted me to build my own version of the fancy joint-making machines I had often admired but had never been able to afford. I based the jig around my joinery needs and the funds I had to work with. And I confess that I arrived at much of the design during some less-than-inspirational philosophy seminars.

The jig I built operates somewhat like the commercially available machines, such as the Matchmaker® or the Multi-Router®, which cost from around $600 to over $1,500. With my jig, the work stays fixed, which means I can move the router with two hands (see the left photo on the facing page) instead of having to manipulate the workpiece, router, and control levers. This makes the jig especially useful at routing the edges of large stock because it's much easier to move the cutter past a piece rather than the other way around. I can also position a template quickly and accurately relative to

the stock, which eliminates much of the trial and error that's required to set up some joint makers.

In addition, the jig's templates are mounted above the router (see the inset photo on the facing page), which makes them easy to see and keeps them away from the dust. Finally, the templates interchange quickly, and their holders easily adapt to different joinery, such as mortises and tenons, finger joints, and dovetails.

Constructing the Jig

Although it may look complicated, my joint-making jig was fairly easy and inexpensive to build (around $160, depending on the amount of work you have done by a machine shop). Basically, the jig is a plunge router mounted horizontally in an upright, linear-motion (X–Y) carriage, which is secured to a frame and table. A following device copies patterns secured by a template holder. I simply clamp the stock to the table and trace the template with the follower as the router cuts the joint.

As shown in the top drawing on p. 74, the jig has five subassemblies: an X–Y carriage, a wooden frame that has a platform and a table, a horizontally adjustable template holder, a vertically adjustable follower, and a fence and hold-down to position and

THE BACK OF THE JIG (inset) reveals a carriage that guides both vertical travel (rods through bushings) and horizontal motion (rails captured by bearings). The router's plunge mechanism sets depth of cut.

THE AUTHOR ROUTS A TENON USING A SHOP-BUILT JIG. Unlike jigs that require an operator to move control levers and machine, this jig fixes the work, which lets you rout with two hands.

clamp stock. I sized the frame to suit my joinery needs, and then I built the rest of the jig around this.

To construct the carriage, you could buy the aluminum bar and flat stock from a metal supplier, but I picked up scrap aluminum for under 70¢ per pound. I cut all the aluminum pieces to length on my table saw fitted with a carbide blade. Then, knowing that I needed a few large holes in the pieces that I couldn't bore with my handheld drill, I took the aluminum to a machine-shop equipped with a CNC mill/drill. The shop performed the work for only $30. Shops with conventional equipment gave me quotes around $100.

Carriage The X–Y carriage consists of two major components: a vertical router carrier and a horizontal roller assembly. The router carrier holds the router and provides up-and-down movement by means of four bronze bushings that ride on two ⅝-in.-dia. steel guide bars. Not expecting ever to have to rout more than 2-in.-thick tenons or dovetails, I allowed just 3½ in. of vertical travel. I mounted the bronze bushings in self-aligning pillow blocks made of stamped steel. The blocks are available from Northern Hydraulics, or you could use linear-motion bearings, which are carried at most bearing-supply shops. The vertical bars are fastened to the horizontal roller assembly, which relies

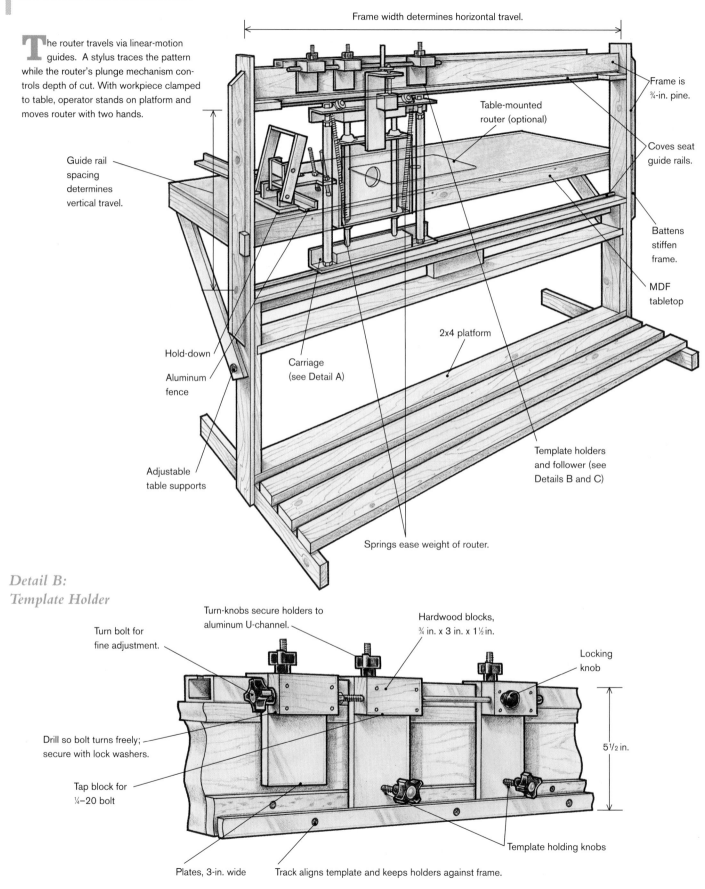

ROUTER JIG ASSEMBLY

The router travels via linear-motion guides. A stylus traces the pattern while the router's plunge mechanism controls depth of cut. With workpiece clamped to table, operator stands on platform and moves router with two hands.

Frame width determines horizontal travel.

Guide rail spacing determines vertical travel.

Table-mounted router (optional)

Frame is ¾-in. pine.

Coves seat guide rails.

Battens stiffen frame.

MDF tabletop

Hold-down

Aluminum fence

Carriage (see Detail A)

2x4 platform

Template holders and follower (see Details B and C)

Adjustable table supports

Springs ease weight of router.

Detail B: Template Holder

Turn bolt for fine adjustment.

Turn-knobs secure holders to aluminum U-channel.

Hardwood blocks, ¾ in. x 3 in. x 1½ in.

Locking knob

Drill so bolt turns freely; secure with lock washers.

Tap block for ¼–20 bolt

5½ in.

Plates, 3-in. wide

Track aligns template and keeps holders against frame.

Template holding knobs

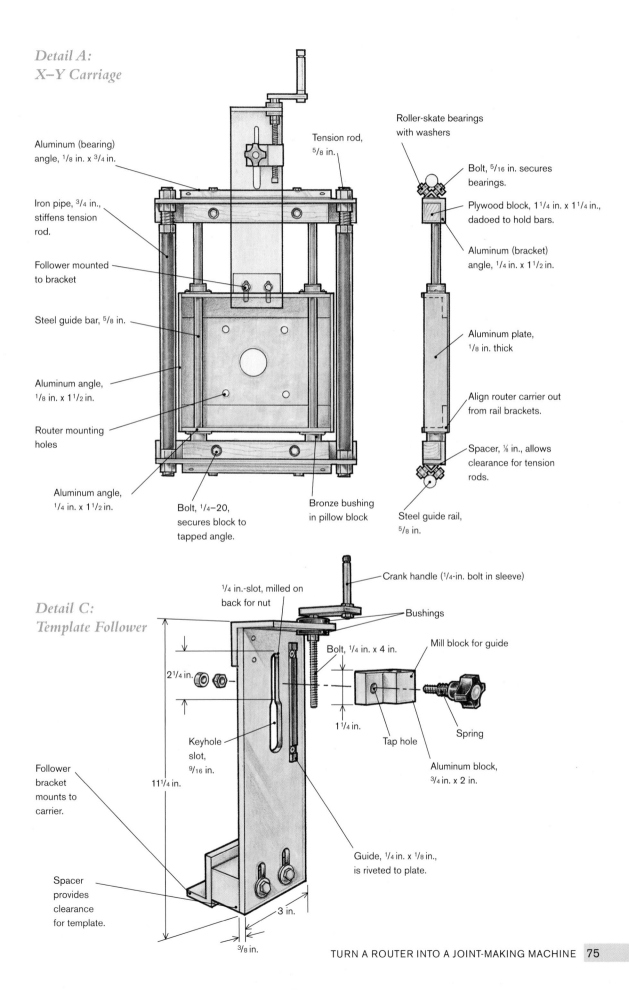

Detail A:
X–Y Carriage

Aluminum (bearing) angle, 1/8 in. x 3/4 in.

Tension rod, 5/8 in.

Roller-skate bearings with washers

Iron pipe, 3/4 in., stiffens tension rod.

Bolt, 5/16 in. secures bearings.

Plywood block, 1 1/4 in. x 1 1/4 in., dadoed to hold bars.

Follower mounted to bracket

Aluminum (bracket) angle, 1/4 in. x 1 1/2 in.

Steel guide bar, 5/8 in.

Aluminum plate, 1/8 in. thick

Aluminum angle, 1/8 in. x 1 1/2 in.

Align router carrier out from rail brackets.

Router mounting holes

Spacer, 1/8 in., allows clearance for tension rods.

Aluminum angle, 1/4 in. x 1 1/2 in.

Bolt, 1/4–20, secures block to tapped angle.

Bronze bushing in pillow block

Steel guide rail, 5/8 in.

Detail C:
Template Follower

1/4 in.-slot, milled on back for nut

Crank handle (1/4-in. bolt in sleeve)

Bushings

Bolt, 1/4 in. x 4 in.

Mill block for guide

2 1/4 in.

1 1/4 in.

Spring

Keyhole slot, 9/16 in.

Tap hole

Follower bracket mounts to carrier.

Aluminum block, 3/4 in. x 2 in.

11 1/4 in.

Spacer provides clearance for template.

Guide, 1/4 in. x 1/8 in., is riveted to plate.

3 in.

3/8 in.

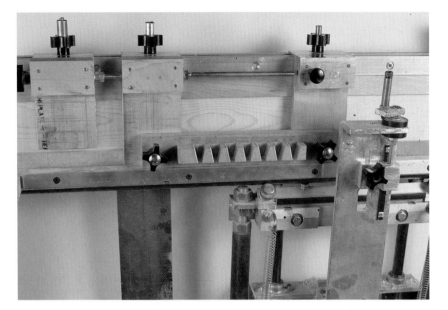

A PATTERN TO FOLLOW. With a template bolted in place, the jig is ready to rout dovetail pins. The template holders (top) are adjustable left and right. The template follower (right) is height adjustable.

on four pairs of precision roller-skate bearings for motion. The bearings are bolted to ¾-in. aluminum-angle brackets. These bearing brackets are fastened to 1½-in. aluminum angles so that the bearings are oriented 45° on either side of two horizontal steel rails (see drawing Detail on p. 75). The bearings and rails work similarly to the guide system I used in a sliding saw table. I used 41-in.-long rails, which allow for 28 in. of horizontal travel.

The router carrier is made from four lengths of 1½-in. aluminum angle riveted together at the corners. I used thicker, ¼-in. angle for the upper and lower pieces of the carrier because they support the bronze bushings. A ⅛-in.-thick aluminum plate mounted between the angles serves as a base for the router and stiffens the assembly. To keep the overall size down, I made the router carrier as small as possible, leaving just enough room for the router base to fit easily between the guide bars. Because the alignment of the bronze bushings is critical, I had their clearance and mounting holes professionally machined.

I connected the bearing-bracket assemblies with two ⅝-in.-dia. by 18-in.-long threaded steel tension rods. The tension rods are stiffened by slightly shorter lengths of ¾-in. iron pipe. I had to cut some of the aluminum angle away so that the inside upper tension-rod nuts could turn freely.

This allows just enough room to adjust the carrier for a tight fit to the guide rails. I secured the vertical guide bars to the horizontal brackets with two ¾-in. plywood mounting plates. I cut the bar-aligning dadoes from a single piece and ripped the two mounting plates from it.

Frame and Table After assembling and mounting the horizontal bearing brackets to the router carrier, I set the tension rods to allow for ½ in. of adjustment either way. Holding the guide rails in place, I measured the outside distance to determine the inside height of the frame. I subtracted ¼ in. from the rail's out-to-out dimension to allow for cove cuts in the frame for the rails. I located the coves so the front of the carrier rides proud of the frame to provide clearance for machining longer stock. The frame width is determined by the length of the horizontal guide rails.

I initially built the frame from ¾-in. pine and later added battens to stiffen the frame. I think a 6/4 hardwood frame would be better. Also, I soon discovered that the frame provides a ledge for chips to build up on, so if I were to build the jig again, I would turn the frame boards on edge and cut bevels on either side of the lower guide rail.

The table is made of pine with a medium-density fiberboard (MDF) top, which can be slid away from the carriage to allow clearance. I also cut holes and slots in the table, so I could mount an aluminum fence and a shopmade hold-down (see the sidebar on the facing page). In the extra table space, I made a cutout for a vertical router (see the photos on p. 73). The lower braces support the table and keep it square to the carriage.

Template Holder and Follower When I designed my machine, I was concerned with providing a way to hold the template and allowing crude lateral adjustments. And I knew that the follower should be rigid and height adjustable. For setup, I initially

A Shopmade Hold-Down

I originally used Jorgensen™ adjustable bar clamps to hold down workpieces on my joint-making jig. But I soon found the repeated tightening and loosening of the clamps to be time-consuming and a real blister maker. I also dismissed the idea of using toggle clamps because of their small size. Instead, I constructed my own clamp using scraps of hard maple, a piece of medium-density fiberboard (MDF) for a base, ⅝-in. threaded rod, dowels, screws and an assortment of ⁵⁄₁₆-in. bolts (see the photos on p. 73).

Building a hold-down is straightforward once you understand the basic operating principle. In the vertical clamp shown in the drawing below, the handle provides leverage to the clamping arm by means of a pivoting bracket, which is fixed between the arm and handle. The clamp locks in place when the handle's pivot point is pulled forward of the arm's pivot. But because clamping pressure diminishes as the arm pivot travels past the initial locking point, a travel-limiting stop is needed. The trick is in placing the stop so that the clamp locks down and exerts sufficient pressure. I arrived at a good balance (favoring clamping strength) by

positioning and paring the block (crossbar) until I was satisfied with the locking action.

Because the forces in the hold-down are mostly vertical, I oriented the grain of the base bracket up and down to prevent splitting. However, because the bracket is screwed to the base, it's possible that the drywall screw could pull out of the bracket's end grain. To counteract this, I reinforced the base brackets with hardwood dowels. Holes drilled through the base enable me to bolt the hold-down to my jig's table. A pair of adjustable spindles with clamping pads resist any side-to-side movement of the workpiece. The spindles are two lengths of ⅝-in. threaded rod with top and bottom nuts. Rubber cap protectors (available at most hardware stores) serve as the pads.

I use my oversize toggle clamp almost exclusively as a hold-down for my router jig, but I sometimes use it as a helping hand when I am power-sanding or freehand-routing. The clamp exerts a lot of down pressure, and I can quickly reposition the stock. The greatest virtue of the clamp, however, is its sheer size. Its long reach and big handle make the clamp truly a pleasure to use in repetitive operations.

Shopmade Hold-Down

*All parts are ¾-in. maple, except base,
which is ¾-in. MDF.*

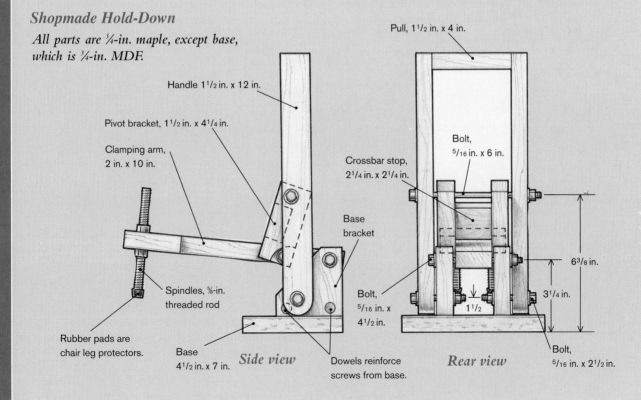

Pull, 1½ in. x 4 in.

Handle 1½ in. x 12 in.

Pivot bracket, 1½ in. x 4¼ in.

Clamping arm,
2 in. x 10 in.

Crossbar stop,
2¼ in. x 2¼ in.

Bolt,
⁵⁄₁₆ in. x 6 in.

Base
bracket

Spindles, ⅝-in.
threaded rod

Bolt,
⁵⁄₁₆ in. x
4½ in.

6³⁄₈ in.

3¼ in.

1½

Rubber pads are
chair leg protectors.

Base
4½ in. x 7 in.

Side view

Dowels reinforce
screws from base.

Rear view

Bolt,
⁵⁄₁₆ in. x 2½ in.

Sources

Northern Hydraulics

2600 17th St. N.E.

Black Eagle, MT 59414

(800) 823-4937

**The Woodworkers'
Store**

21801 Industrial Blvd.

Rogers, Minn. 55374-
9514

612-428-2199

Garrett Wade Co.

161 Avenue of the
Americas

New York, N.Y. 10013

800-221-2942

Prices here are
estimates from 1993.

relied on a cut and nudge method: Take a trial cut, estimate the error and nudge either the template or follower to compensate. But it didn't take long to produce a pile of waste tenons that way.

To remedy this situation, I introduced screw-driven adjusting mechanisms into both the template holder and the follower (see Details B and C on pp. 74 and 75). The template holders consist of three brackets constructed from ¼-in. aluminum plate and 1½-in. angle. The brackets can be individually locked to a guide track by turn-knobs (available from The Woodworkers' Store℠).

The two right brackets are joined by a rod that adjusts for different-sized templates, and both are tapped for ¼–20 screws to mount the templates. The left bracket is fitted with a free-turning bolt that connects it with the template holders. Locking the left bracket only and turning the adjustment bolt moves the template .05 in. per turn. Recently, I got my hands on some FastTrack aluminum extrusions (available from Garrett Wade Company), which when combined with their microadjuster and two microblocks made a nearly ready-to-use template holder.

For the template follower, I had to add a means of inserting the bearing into the mortise template, so I devised a keyhole-shaped slot (see the photo on p. 76). After the follower bearing is slid into the narrow slot, it can then be cranked reliably, up or down, into position.

Routing Mortises and Tenons

Unlike the Leigh® dovetail router jig, which uses adjustable templates, my jig has interchangeable templates. I make my templates from scraps of medium-density fiberboard (see the photo at left below) because it is dimensionally stable, wears well and is easy to work. I make the mortise template first and then shape the tenon template to fit snugly into a test mortise. This is necessary because of the bearing system I use. Instead of ball bearings, I used a bronze bearing that slips on the ¼-in. follower shaft. I matched a ¼-in. mortising bit to a ⁵⁄₁₆-in. bronze bearing. This combination produces mortises that are slightly smaller than the template, so I fit the tenons to the mortise rather than to the template.

I usually eyeball the position of the template by first marking the stock, clamping it

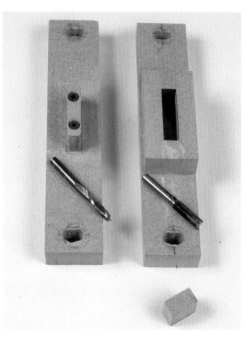

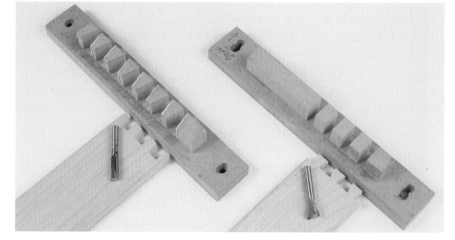

MATCHING TEMPLATES AND BITS–As a sample of the jig's versatility, the author displays mated templates and corresponding bits. For adjustment, the mortise-and-tenon pattern (left) has a screw-on tenon and a mortise-shortening insert. The pin-and-dovetail templates produced the joinery examples above. When indexed by the tail pattern, the jig can also cut finger joints; simply swap a straight router bit for the dovetail bit.

in place, and then positioning the template holder and follower so that the router bit just grazes my layout lines. Then I'll take a shallow test cut and measure the location with dial calipers. When I cut the stock, the surfaces that will be exposed are face down. I adjust the horizontal position by locking the left template bracket and turning the adjustment screw to move the template. I measure with my dial calipers to compensate for exactly half of the initial error. A similar technique adjusts the follower vertically.

When cutting mortises, the end of the stock bears against the router carrier. The edge is clamped against the fence with the hold-down. An aluminum plate fastened to the upper frame and scribed with a vertical indicator line marks the center of the cut. To lay out my mortises, I mark their center and align them with the indicator.

To cut the tenons, I bolt on a tenon template and change over to a ½-in. straight bit. I climb-cut the first pass, which virtually eliminates any tearout and provides a very clean shoulder line. I complete the cut by merely following the template until no more shavings are produced. The X–Y carriage isn't stiff enough to entirely resist deflection, so I have learned merely to follow the template rather than force the follower bearing against it. I test-fit each piece immediately after machining, and I correct a too-tight fit by exerting a little more force during the cut.

Routing Dovetails and Pins

My joint-making jig handles through-dovetails (see the photo at right) as easily as it does mortises and tenons. But making a set of dovetail templates is a bit more involved. The main trick is getting the spacing of the pin template to exactly match that of the tails. The tail template is really just a spacing guide, resembling half of a finger joint. In addition to getting the spacing and cut angle right, the pins of the

template must be left full enough to ensure a tightly fitting joint. Also, by making the template at least twice as wide as the thickness of the stock, you can adjust the fit of the joint simply by changing the vertical position of the router bit on the stock. Because the height is relative to the template, it's easy to adjust the vertical position of the follower.

I've adapted Mark Duginske's method for cutting dovetail templates on the tablesaw. I use a set of wooden blocks to establish the spacing of the dado cuts. After cutting the tail template, I use the same set of blocks to machine the pin template. With this method, you can also make templates for nonuniformly spaced joints as long as you number and order both templates.

Always cut the tails first, using whatever dovetail bit the template is designed for (see the right photo on the facing page). I place a piece of stock flat against the router carrier to set the depth of cut, extending the bit just proud of the piece, and clamp the stock face down. I adjust the template holders horizontally and position the cut so the outside tails are equidistant from the edges of the board.

I fit my router with a straight bit for machining the pins. I mount the template and position the stock so that the inside of the joint faces down. This arrangement ensures that once everything is adjusted, slight variations in stock thickness will not affect the joint's fit. The fit is determined by the distance between the follower and the bit—smaller distances will yield tighter joints and vice versa. With a test piece clamped in place (and the router unplugged), I position the follower so that the bit is just below the workpiece when the follower first contacts the bottom of the template. From here, I make test cuts and raise the follower.

MACHINE-CUT JOINT SPEAKS FOR ITSELF. The author holds a drawer corner of oiled cherry and maple, dovetailed with the router jig. The jig cuts uniform dovetails or asymmetrical ones, if a hand-cut look is desired.

GUY PEREZ is studying political philosophy in Madison, Wisconsin. He also builds furniture for his family and friends.

Make Your Own Dovetail Jig

BY WILLIAM H. PAGE

The blanket chest I wanted to make for a gift was basically a large box joined with dovetails at the corners. I didn't have enough time to hand-cut the joints, and I didn't want to pay $300 for a commercial jig to do the job, so I set to work developing my own jig.

Shop-built from scraps, these unusual jigs, one for the tails and one for the pins, cut tight-fitting through-dovetails (see the photo below), a task that even many commercial jigs can't handle. Designed for routing dovetails for large carcase construction, the jigs can be built in less than two hours for just pennies.

Layout is quite simple and can be done as the tail jig is being assembled. Fingers screwed to the tail jig guide the router bits; the key is ball bearings. The bits used to cut the joint are guided by bearings the same

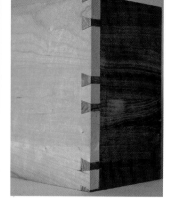

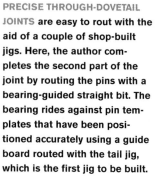

PRECISE THROUGH-DOVETAIL JOINTS are easy to rout with the aid of a couple of shop-built jigs. Here, the author completes the second part of the joint by routing the pins with a bearing-guided straight bit. The bearing rides against pin templates that have been positioned accurately using a guide board routed with the tail jig, which is the first jig to be built.

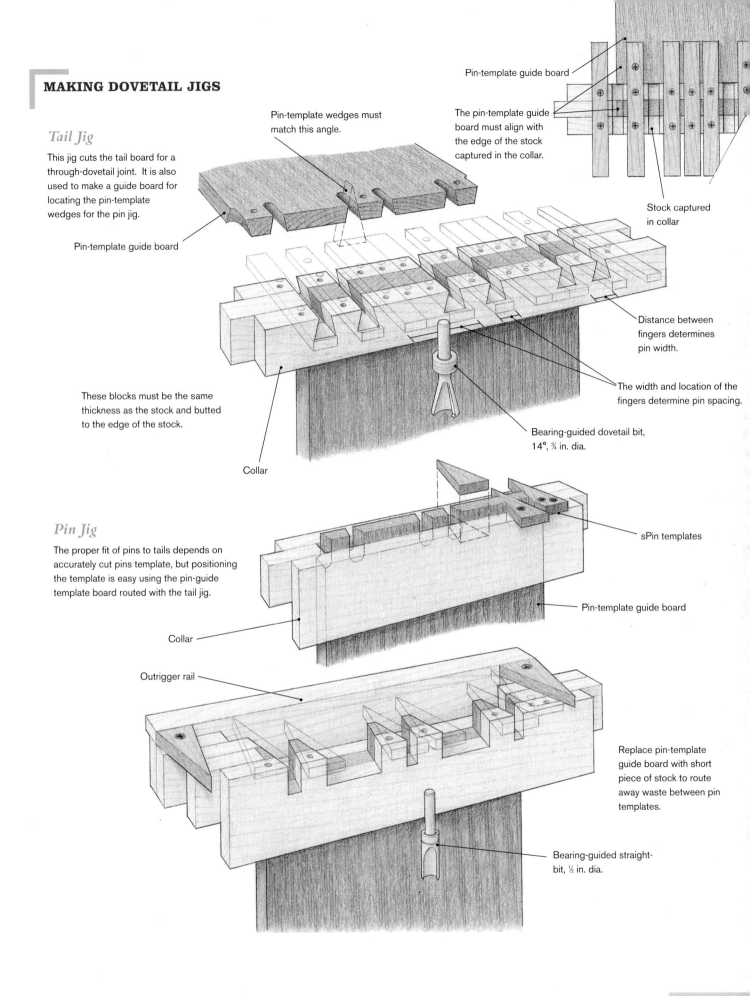

MAKING DOVETAIL JIGS

Tail Jig

This jig cuts the tail board for a through-dovetail joint. It is also used to make a guide board for locating the pin-template wedges for the pin jig.

Pin-template guide board

Pin-template wedges must match this angle.

Pin-template guide board

The pin-template guide board must align with the edge of the stock captured in the collar.

Stock captured in collar

Distance between fingers determines pin width.

The width and location of the fingers determine pin spacing.

Bearing-guided dovetail bit, 14°, ¾ in. dia.

These blocks must be the same thickness as the stock and butted to the edge of the stock.

Collar

Pin Jig

The proper fit of pins to tails depends on accurately cut pins template, but positioning the template is easy using the pin-guide template board routed with the tail jig.

sPin templates

Pin-template guide board

Collar

Outrigger rail

Replace pin-template guide board with short piece of stock to route away waste between pin templates.

Bearing-guided straight-bit, ½ in. dia.

diameter as the cutter. Pin and tail size and spacing are variable, and jigs can be built to handle any width board.

Basics of Jig Construction

Before making any of the jigs, the project stock must be jointed, planed, and cut to final dimensions. The stock should be flat and square, and be sure to include a couple extra feet of stock for making and testing the jigs. The jigs are assembled around some scraps cut from the actual stock. This way, the jigs precisely fit the stock and eliminate the need to fiddle with adjustments or set-up routines, ensuring perfect-fitting dovetails.

I start with the tail jig; and in the process of making this jig, I also cut a guide board that precisely locates the pin templates for assembling the pin jig. Using the tail jig to rout the pin-template guide board ensures a perfect match of pins to tails.

The tail jig consists of a collar that surrounds the stock to be joined and a series of fingers screwed to the top of this collar, as shown in the drawings on p. 81. The fingers serve as a stop when inserting stock into the collar and as a guide for the bearing on the bit. The location of these fingers across the top of the collar determines the spacing of the pins.

With the fingers in place, I run the dovetail bit through the collar of the jig and a scrap piece of stock clamped in the jig. These cuts create the tail piece, or the openings that the pins will fit into, and prepare the jig for use. The collar must be clamped to the stock to avoid any movement that could affect the accuracy of the cut.

The pin jig consists of a collar built around the pin-template guide board, but instead of straight fingers, the pin templates for this jig are wedges with an included angle to match the cut of the dovetail bit. An outrigger attached to the pin collar provides full support for the router when routing the pins.

With both jigs assembled, I rout a joint in a couple of pieces of scrap clamped firmly in the collars to test the fit and to be sure I like the pattern before proceeding with my good stock.

Making the Tail Jig

To make the tail jig (see the drawings on p. 81), I clamp a short piece of the prepared stock in my bench vise. I begin by building the collar around this piece of stock, using 2-in.- to 3-in.-wide scraps that are about 4 in. longer than the width of the stock. The collar pieces are clamped flush to the end of the stock so that they overhang equally on both sides of the stock. The end collar blocks should be butted tightly to the side of the stock.

The guide fingers that are glued and screwed to the top of the collar are simply strips of hardwood or plywood about ⅜ in. thick and about 8 in. long. Position the strips for any pin pattern that you want, but keep in mind that the pins must be at least ¾ in. wide, the diameter of the bearing that will ride against the fingers. Also, the distance between the pins must be at least equal to the diameter of the straight bit used to cut the pins. The fingers also must be square to the collar. To avoid pin cutouts where I don't want them, I fill gaps between the fingers.

To rout the tail jig, I chuck my bearing-equipped dovetail bit in the router and set the depth of cut about 1/32 in. deeper than the thickness of my prepared stock. (Bearing guided bits can be made by gluing a bearing the same size as the bit to the bit's shaft, or they can be ordered from Freud Company.) I then rout the tails by running the bearing between the fingers. I make two passes in each slot to be sure the bearing rides firmly against both fingers for each pin cutout or else the pins won't align properly with the tails. This completes the tail jig, and in the process, I've made a scrap tail piece to test the fit of the joint.

Making the Pin Jig

The first step in making the pin jig is to use the tail jig for cutting the guide that locates the pin templates, so the pins and tails line up. I do this by butting a piece of prepared stock against the back side of the tail collar and screwing down through the fingers and into the jig stock. This piece of stock must be the same width as the workpieces to be joined, and its edges must align with the edges of the jig (see the drawings on p. 81). To create the pin guide, I run my router between the fingers of the tail jig as before, cutting approximately an inch into the stock. After routing, I unscrew the pin guide and then clamp it in my bench vise with the routed end up.

As with the tail jig, I build a four-piece collar around the pin guide clamped in the vise. I let the pin guide extend about 1/2 in. above the collar, so the routed slots can be used to position the pin templates on the collar.

The pin templates are 5/8-in.-thick wedges that I cut on the tablesaw from a long strip about 3 in. wide. I set my miter gauge to 14° (because I used a 14° dovetail bit), cut one edge of the wedge, flip the strip over, and then cut the other edge of the wedge. I test-fit the wedge into the pin guide, make minor adjustments to the

miter gauge as necessary, and then cut a new wedge. I continue this process until I get a wedge that fits snugly into the pin guide with no gaps on either edge (see the drawings on p. 81). Then I cut a wedge, or pin template, for each slot in the pin guide.

I then push the pin templates firmly into place on the pin guide and glue and screw the templates to the collar. To fully support the router, I needed to attach an outrigger rail to the collar in front of the pointed end of the templates.

To route the pins, I set up a second router with a bearing-guided, 1/2-in.-dia. straight bit. Again, the depth of cut is just a hair deeper than the thickness of the stock. Before routing away the waste between the pins, I remove the pin-template guide board from the jig and replace it with a short piece of the prepared stock. Then, with the router sitting on the pin templates and the outrigger rail, I route away all the material on the collars and the scrap stock that is not covered by the pin templates. I used firm pressure to be sure the bearing rode tightly against the templates for an accurate cut. Routing the waste completes the jig and cuts a pin test piece.

I remove the test piece and try it in the tails previously cut. If the joint is too loose or too tight, it's usually a result of not keeping the guide bearing firmly against the sides of the fingers or pin templates. You might want to try running the router through the jigs again with new test pieces in place. Minor misfits can be adjusted by shaving the edge of the pin templates or adding masking-tape shims. If you're satisfied with the fit and spacing, slide the appropriate jig over the end of your stock and start cutting. The actual routing of the joints takes about five minutes each.

WILLIAM PAGE is a woodworker in Toledo, Ohio.

Sources

Freud
218 Feld Ave.
High Point, N.C. 27264

Shopmade Dovetail Templates

BY JAMIE BUXTON

Hand-cut dovetails are versatile and suitable for projects of any size. The problem, however, is that they're time-consuming to make and require a fair amount of skill. Router jigs solve some of the problems, but the most adaptable jigs cost a lot of money. It turns out that there's another solution: custom-size shopmade router templates.

I worked on the problem in my spare time, and after a few weeks of number crunching, I was ready to put my theory to the test. In a few hours I succeeded in making my first dovetailed drawer using a pair of shopmade templates.

My method is limited to making variably spaced, half-blind dovetails. Both halves of the joint are cut using a bearing-guided dovetail bit. Then I ease the corners of the square-cornered tails with a chisel so that they fit the round-cornered sockets. With this method I can cut joints faster than I could by hand, yet it allows me to custom-make templates for individual projects.

Half-blind dovetails are most commonly used to join drawer sides and fronts, but you can also use them to join solid casework. My templates take only an hour or so to build, and I make a new set for each project so that the dovetail pattern is perfectly suited to the width and scale of the piece.

Accurate by Construction

My system uses two templates—one for cutting tails and another for cutting pins. Because the initial and critical machining for the templates is done with them sandwiched together, they are mirror images of each other, which makes the joint accurate.

As with all machine-cut dovetail joints, tails cannot be any narrower than the dovetail bit itself. But the maximum width of the tails and the maximum spacing between them are infinitely variable, features that make this technique so versatile.

These jigs have their idiosyncrasies. For example, the height of the tails depends on the thickness of the sawblade used to make the first cuts in the template (see the chart on p. 87).

To join ¾-in.-thick stock and end up with ½-in.-high tails, which look about right, I use an 8° ¹¹⁄₁₆-in.-dia. dovetail bit fitted with a ¾-in.-dia. bearing. Next, lay out the tails on the stock, keeping in mind the diameter of the dovetail bit at its widest point. Then transfer those marks to the tails template. Clamp both templates together so that they are flush on all sides.

Before making a first template, make some test cuts in scrap using whatever sawblades are available. Measure the kerf with a dial caliper, then refer to the chart. You may

THE VARIABLE-SPACED, HALF-BLIND DOVETAIL JOINT IS COMPLETE. **Templates can be custom-made for any project of any width.**

find that the measurements (kerf widths) don't exactly match my chart. Don't worry. Find the closest match and make a template that suits your needs. It can be fine-tuned later. I use a blade that's a hair thicker than ⅛ in., but it produces a kerf of 0.135 in. due to runout.

Template stock should be about 6 in. wide so that it can support a router and slightly longer than the workpiece to allow for clamps. I use plywood or medium-density fiberboard (MDF) for the templates and laminate the material to get stock that is at least 1 in. thick. Both templates must be the same thickness.

Clamp the tails and pins templates together and lay out the dovetails. The space between the fingers on the tails template must, obviously, be larger than the diameter of the bit's pilot bearing. Next, using the

Making the Templates

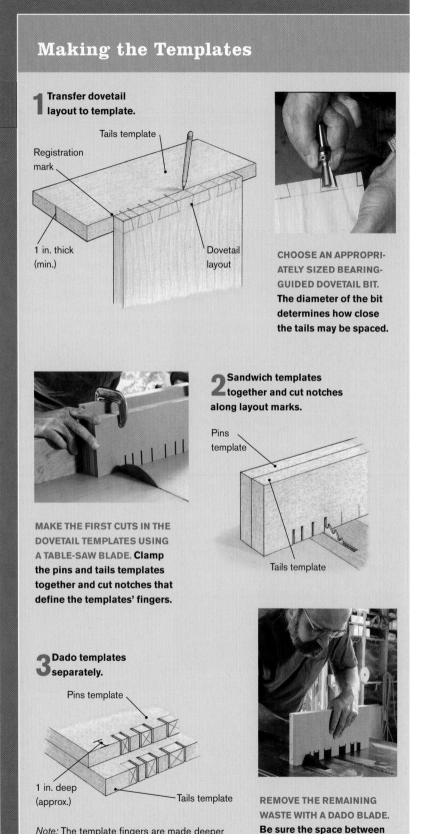

1 Transfer dovetail layout to template.

Tails template

Registration mark

1 in. thick (min.)

Dovetail layout

CHOOSE AN APPROPRIATELY SIZED BEARING-GUIDED DOVETAIL BIT. The diameter of the bit determines how close the tails may be spaced.

2 Sandwich templates together and cut notches along layout marks.

Pins template

Tails template

MAKE THE FIRST CUTS IN THE DOVETAIL TEMPLATES USING A TABLE-SAW BLADE. Clamp the pins and tails templates together and cut notches that define the templates' fingers.

3 Dado templates separately.

Pins template

1 in. deep (approx.)

Tails template

Note: The template fingers are made deeper than necessary. The extra depth allows you to adjust the offsets, if necessary, to get snug-fitting dovetail joints.

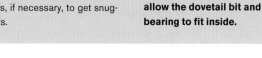

REMOVE THE REMAINING WASTE WITH A DADO BLADE. Be sure the space between fingers is wide enough to allow the dovetail bit and bearing to fit inside.

tablesaw, cut out notches along the layout lines. Make these notches deeper than the depth of the tails by about ½ in. (The exact amount isn't important; you'll see why soon.) Separate the halves and mark out the waste sections, which will be opposite for each half. Finally, remove the waste with a dado blade set for a slightly shallower cut than the notches. The exact depth of cut is not important as long as it's greater than the height of the tails (refer to the chart). For the ¹¹⁄₁₆-in.-dia. dovetail bit, I cut a dado that's about 1 in. deep.

Mark out the offsets on both the pins and tails templates. The offsets are used to register stock. Because the dadoes on the templates are cut deep, the offsets can be repositioned, if necessary, to tweak the fit of the joint. One could make the templates without offsets for an exact fit, but it's not worth the extra effort.

I mark the offsets using a finely sharpened mechanical pencil. For the pins template, measure the offset from the bottom of the dado out toward the edge of the template. For the tails template, do the opposite: Measure the offset from the outside edge of the template in toward the base of the dado. Offsets will vary, depending on the thickness of the stock and the kerf width (see the chart on p. 87).

Finally, screw a backer board onto the tails template. I use a piece of 2x4 that has been jointed square. The block does two things: It registers the stock to the offset and prevents tearout as the bit exits the tails stock. The pins template requires no additional preparation.

Using the Templates

Chuck the bit in the router and set the depth. Refer to the chart and be sure to add the thickness of the template to the depth setting. Some routers with limited travel may not work with my templates. I use a 3¼-hp plunge router that has lots of travel. Use the same depth setting for cutting both pins and tails.

Now for the fine-tuning. If your saw's kerf is a few thousandths of an inch wider than indicated in the chart, set the router bit slightly deeper. Conversely, if your saw leaves a kerf thinner than indicated in the chart, set the bit shallower by a few thousandths of an inch. Make trial cuts in scrap and check the fit. If the joint is loose, adjust the router for a deeper cut.

To make the cuts, secure the tails stock—with the inside face out—to the tails template using a pair of clamps. Place the stock in a vise to hold it upright. Take a light pass along the edge of the board to establish the shoulder cut. Then rout out the remaining waste, taking care that the router-bit bearing rides firmly along the fingers of the template. Make a second pass to ensure a clean cut. If you are using a ¼-in.-dia. shank bit, remove most of the waste using a straight bit first to avoid stressing the dovetail bit. I prefer to use ½-in.-dia. shank bits whenever possible.

The pins template is clamped to the inside face of the stock, which is aligned to the offset. I clamp the template and stock directly to my workbench with a second pair of clamps. Make the cuts, moving the router from left to right. If your router seems to be straining, especially when cutting thick stock, take several light passes.

Because the tails have square corners and the pins have rounded corners, they won't seat properly. I solve that by chopping off the corners of the tails using a chisel. The corners need not be rounded to match the pins perfectly because most of the joint's strength will be in the long-grained areas. But if you prefer, the pins can be chiseled out and made square to mate cleanly with the tails.

JAMIE BUXTON is a computer engineer and woodworker who lives in Redwood City, California.

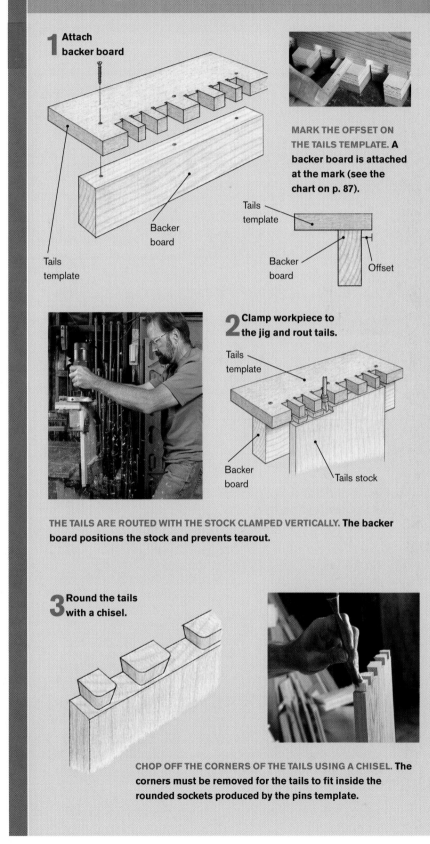

Routing the Tails

1 Attach backer board

MARK THE OFFSET ON THE TAILS TEMPLATE. **A backer board is attached at the mark (see the chart on p. 87).**

Tails template

Backer board

Tails template

Backer board

Offset

2 Clamp workpiece to the jig and rout tails.

Tails template

Backer board

Tails stock

THE TAILS ARE ROUTED WITH THE STOCK CLAMPED VERTICALLY. **The backer board positions the stock and prevents tearout.**

3 Round the tails with a chisel.

CHOP OFF THE CORNERS OF THE TAILS USING A CHISEL. **The corners must be removed for the tails to fit inside the rounded sockets produced by the pins template.**

DOVETAIL TEMPLATE SETTINGS

Cutter diameter (inches)	Cutter angle (degrees)	Bearing diameter (inches)	Kerf width (inches)	Depth setting* (inches)	Offsets ½-in. stock (inches)		Offsets ⅝-in. stock (inches)		Offsets ¾-in. stock (inches)	
					Tails	Pins	Tails	Pins	Tails	Pins
11⁄16	8	¾	0.125	0.445						
11⁄16	8	¾	0.135	0.516	0.344	0.469	0.469	0.594	0.656	0.781
11⁄16	8	¾	0.160	0.694	0.334	0.469	0.459	0.594	0.646	0.781
11⁄16	8	¾	0.200	0.978	0.309	0.469	0.434	0.594	0.621	0.781
					0.269	0.469	0.394	0.594	0.581	0.781

*Add this number to the thickness of the template for the actual router-bit depth setting. For an expanded chart, see our Web site at www.finewoodworking.com.

Routing the Pins

1 Mark offset on pins template.

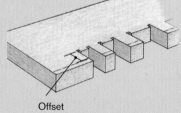

Pins template

Offset

USE A RULER TO MARK THE OFFSET. The pins offset will depend on the thickness of the stock used (see the chart above).

2 Clamp workpiece at offset line and rout pins.

THE PINS STOCK IS CLAMPED FACEDOWN TO THE TEMPLATE. Rout the pins from above using a router bit with a bearing and stop collar.

Sources

Eagle America
800-872-2511
www.eagle-america.com
offers a good selection of dovetail bits, including 8° bits, which I use frequently. Eagle also sells bearings and stop collars, which are needed with my templates. The collar and bearing fit directly over the bit's shank.

Compact Tool Makes Dadoes a Snap

BY SKIP LAUDERBAUGH

Many of my cabinetmaking projects require panels that have dadoes, rabbets, and grooves to allow strong, easy assembly. I've tried lots of ways of cutting these joints and have found that a panel router is the quickest and most accurate tool to use. Unfortunately, the expense of one of the commercial machines (up to $3,500) and the floor space it requires (up to 25 sq. ft.) are more than I can justify. As is often the case, however, once you have tasted using the proper tool for a particular job, using anything else becomes a frustrating compromise.

I had seen other shopmade panel routers, but they lacked features I wanted and seemed complicated. So I set out to design and build my own version of a panel router. By simplifying the guide system and by using common materials and hardware (see the drawing on p. 93), I built a panel router for less than $100 (not including the router, which I already owned). And although this jig easily handles big pieces of plywood and melamine, the jig folds compactly against the wall when it is not in use.

Designing the Panel Router

Because the guide rails used in industrial panel routers often get in the way, the rails were the first things I eliminated on my design. The next thing was to orient the machine so that gravity would help feed the router into the work. Big panel routers are oriented horizontally, and they have the capacity to handle 36-in.-wide pieces of plywood. But because shelf dadoes in cabinets and cases are usually less than 3 ft. wide, I scaled things down a bit, and I situated the whole setup vertically. This orientation also saved considerable shop space. Then I came up with a clamp-on router guidance system,

WALL-MOUNTED PANEL ROUTER IS IDEAL FOR MAKING QUICK DADOES. **Knowing his panel router had to save space, the author mounted it to a wall at a comfortable height and angle. To build the jig, he used a router he owned and commercial hardware costing less than $100.**

THE KEY TO THE ROUTER GUIDE
IS INTERLOCKING ALUMINUM
TRACK. **When the author discovered the edges of Clamp 'N Tool
Guides nest and slide easily, he
made them into a two-piece
guide system: An inverted 21-in.
piece is fixed to the router subbase, and another piece is
clamped to the work.**

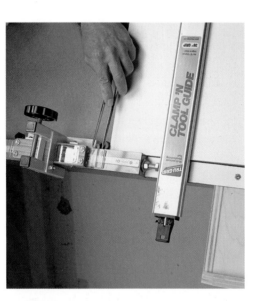

THE FENCE'S ADJUSTABLE STOP
ENSURES PERFECT ALIGNMENT.
**A Biesemeyer micro-adjustable
stop and measuring system
precisely positions the left side
of the work for each dado or
groove. The author uses a pair
of dividers to point out two cur-
sors that indicate left and right
limits of a cut.**

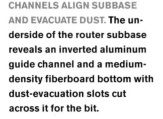

CHANNELS ALIGN SUBBASE
AND EVACUATE DUST. **The underside of the router subbase
reveals an inverted aluminum
guide channel and a medium-
density fiberboard bottom with
dust-evacuation slots cut
across it for the bit.**

so I don't have to do any measuring or marking on a panel. Finally, I devised a router subbase that eliminates depth-of-cut adjustments
when changing material thicknesses. To help
you understand the abilities of this tool and
how it is constructed, I've divided it into six
basic components:

1. The workpiece table
2. The router guide system
3. The fence with adjustable stop
4. The upper and lower guide stops
5. The router subbase
6. The router tray

The Workpiece Table A panel router requires a flat, stable work surface with a
straight edge for mounting the fence. I
chose an ordinary 3-ft.-wide hollow core
door for the table because it provides those
things, and at $15, it cost less than what I
could build it for. I mounted the table to a
ledger on the wall. The ledger is 75 in. from
the floor to give a comfortable working
height. A 5-in. space from the wall gives
enough clearance for the guide system.
Standard door hinges let the table swing
out of the way for storage, and side supports hold the table at a 65° angle when the
table is in use.

The Router Guide System Several years
ago, I discovered that the aluminum extrusions used in Tru-Grip's® Clamp 'N Tool
Guides® interlock when one is inverted
(see the bottom photo at left). In this configuration, the two pieces slide smoothly
back and forth with little side play, like a
track. This system has several benefits: A
panel can be set directly on the table without having to go under fixed guide rails.
The guide is accurately located, and the
panel is clamped tightly to the fence and
to the table. The clamps are available in
several lengths, but I've found that 36 in.
is the most convenient. The manufacturer
recommends using silicone spray to minimize wear.

The Fence with Adjustable Stop The fence holds the bottom edge of a panel straight, adds a runner for an adjustable stop and measuring system, and gives a place to mount the lower guide stop. Fence construction is partially dictated by the stop you use. I chose a Biesemeyer® miter stop because it has two adjustable hairline pointers, which let you set and read both sides of a dado (see the top photo on the facing page).

For the adjustable stop to work, the fence should be 1½ in. thick and the top edge of the fence has to be 1⅝ in. above the top of the table. My fence is two thicknesses of ¾-in. plywood laminated to form a 1½-in.-thick piece that is 3 in. wide and 96 in. long. To allow the router to pass through at the end of a cut, I made a 1-in.-deep notch in the fence. The notch is 13 in. long to fit my router. I located this notch 36 in. from the right, so I can dado in the center of an 8-ft.-long panel. To finish off the fence, I glued plastic laminate to the top, faces, and ends. Before mounting, I cut a ¼-in. by ¼-in. groove in the back to provide for dust clearance, which ensures that the bottom of a panel stays flush to the fence. The fence is mounted to the bottom edge of the table with 2½-in.-long screws.

The Upper and Lower Guide Stops The upper and lower guide stops allow the Clamp'N Tool Guide to be set exactly 90° to the bottom edge of a panel. The lower guide stop is integrated in the fence (see the top photo on the facing page), and the upper guide stop is fixed to the top of the table. The lower stop is a ⅜-in. bolt threaded into a T-nut inset into a block and glued to a notch in the fence. The center of the bolt head should be 1⅛ in. above the work surface, or ½ in. above the bottom of the notch. The upper stop consists of two pieces of ¾-in.-thick plywood laminated to form a 1½-in.-thick piece, 12 in. long. The top is notched on both ends to leave a 2-in.- by 2½-in.-wide section in the center. Another

bolt and T-nut are screwed to the shoulder. The center of this bolt is 1⅛ in. above the bottom of the notch. To fine-tune the stops for square, turn the bolts, and lock them with a nut. After the stops are set, adhere the measuring tape for the adjustable stops onto the top of the fence.

The Router Subbase Parts for the router subbase consist of a medium-density fiberboard (MDF) bottom, an upper base made out of ¾-in. plywood that mounts to the router, and a piece of upside-down extrusion screwed to the side so it can engage

Commercial Bits Make Clear Cuts

Commercial panel routers work so well because the router bits are specifically designed to eliminate chipping and tearout, and they can also cut at higher feed rates. But their biggest benefit is that their cutter and arbor are two separate pieces (see the photo at right), which means that the arbor can stay secured in the router collet while you simply unscrew the cutter from the ½-in. arbor to change the bit size.

Commercial panel-router bits (see Sources on p. 92) are available in a full range of sizes, including undersize ones for veneer plywood and oversize ones for two-sided melamine. An arbor and cutter set costs about $35, less than a decent-quality dado blade set.

When you need to change the width of a dado, select the correct cutter size, and screw it on the arbor (no wrenches required). The depth of cut doesn't need to be

PANEL-ROUTING BITS CHANGE EASILY. **The only things the author uses from industrial panel routers are the bits, which have interchangeable cutter tips.**

reset because the height of the cutter stays the same. This process is much quicker than using a dado blade on the table saw, where you have to use shims to get the proper width and then make test cuts to set the depth of cut.

the guide track. Drawing Detail B (facing page) shows the dimensions I used to mount my Porter-Cable model 690 router. But you could modify the subbase to suit your router. Regardless of the router, the bottom should be ⅜ in. thick so that the extrusions interlock properly.

After the bottom is cut to size, center the baseplate on the bottom and align the router handles at a right angle to the extrusion. Drill and countersink the mounting holes and mount the upper base to the bottom. Next, carefully, plunge a ¾-in. bit by slowly lowering the router motor. Then cut two dadoes, each ¼ in. deep by ¾ in. wide across the bottom. The first dado runs the full length and the second goes halfway across, 90° to the first. This T-shaped slot removes dust from the subbase (see the center photo on p. 90).

For the piece of inverted extrusion, I obtained stock from the manufacturer. But because they currently don't sell this separately, just buy a 24-in. clamp, and cut off the ends. I used a 21-in.-long piece.

The bottom of the router subbase slides directly on the face of the panel so that the depth of cut is registered from the top of the panel. This is desirable because when you switch material thickness from ⅜ in. to ¾ in., for example, the depth of cut does not have to be adjusted. Also, if the panel is

slightly warped or some dust gets between the panel and the table, the cutting depth is not affected. Interchangeable bits also speed up the process (see the sidebar on p. 91).

The Router Tray The purpose of the router tray is to give the router a place to rest after it has completed a cut. The tray is mounted to the fence on the back side of the notched-out area. My tray is made out of ¾-in. plywood and is screwed to the fence. On the right edge of the tray, a piece of ⅛-in. Plexiglas® protrudes into the tray opening. As the router slides down into the tray, the Plexiglas piece fits into a slot cut into the edge of the subbase and prevents the router from lifting out of the tray.

Using the Panel Router

The panel-router sequence to make a dado goes like this: First, I set the adjustable stop to locate the dado where I want it. Second, I set the panel on the table and slide it up against the adjustable stop. Third, I place the Clamp 'N Tool Guide on the panel, slide it against the upper and lower guide stops, and clamp it down (see the photo at left). In this one step, the guide is squared to the panel and clamped to the table. Fourth, I set the router on the panel with the extrusions interlocked. I hold the router subbase above the top of the panel so the bit clears. Finally, I turn the router on and cut the dado. To make stop dadoes, I insert a spacer block in the bottom of the tray to prevent the router from cutting all the way across a panel. While this setup may not be perfect for a large production shop, it is certainly affordable and conserves space.

SKIP LAUDERBAUGH is a sales representative for Blum hardware and a college woodworking instructor. His shop is in Costa Mesa, California.

SETUP FOR DADOES IS EASY. Just slide the Clamp 'N Tool Guide to the stops, and clamp the guide to the work by snugging up the black plastic dogs.

PANEL-ROUTER ASSEMBLY

Panel router handles common sheet thickness, stores flat against wall, and folds out for use.

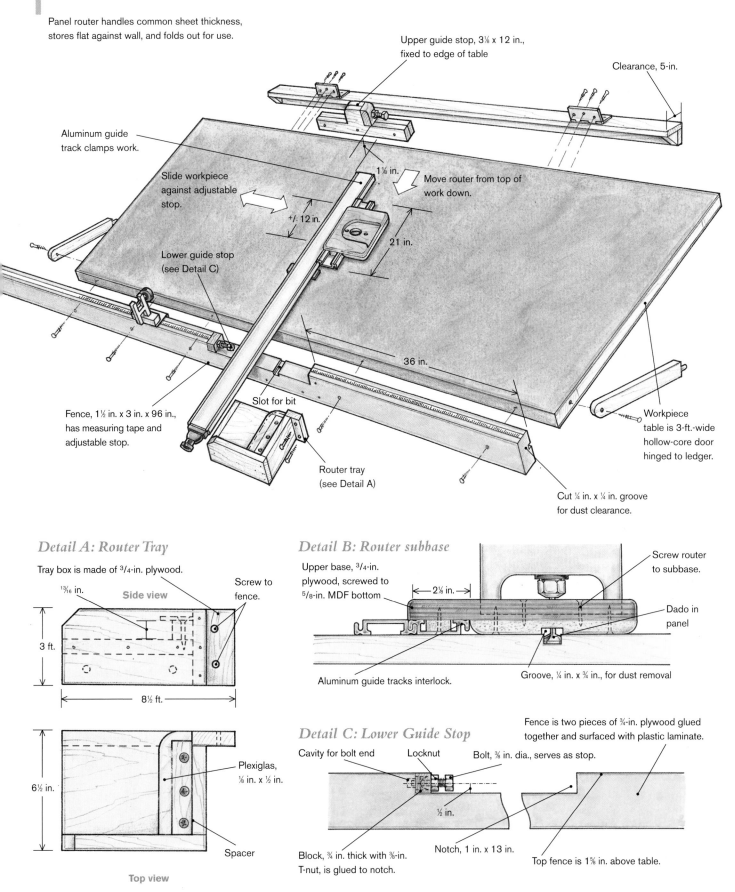

Upper guide stop, 3⅛ x 12 in., fixed to edge of table

Clearance, 5-in.

Aluminum guide track clamps work.

Slide workpiece against adjustable stop.

1⅛ in.

Move router from top of work down.

+/- 12 in.

21 in.

Lower guide stop (see Detail C)

36 in.

Fence, 1½ in. x 3 in. x 96 in., has measuring tape and adjustable stop.

Slot for bit

Router tray (see Detail A)

Workpiece table is 3-ft.-wide hollow-core door hinged to ledger.

Cut ¼ in. x ¼ in. groove for dust clearance.

Detail A: Router Tray

Tray box is made of ³/₄-in. plywood.

Side view

1³/₁₆ in.

3 ft.

Screw to fence.

8½ ft.

6½ in.

Plexiglas, ⅛ in. x ½ in.

Spacer

Top view

Detail B: Router subbase

Upper base, ³/₄-in. plywood, screwed to ⅝-in. MDF bottom

2⅛ in.

Screw router to subbase.

Dado in panel

Aluminum guide tracks interlock.

Groove, ¼ in. x ¾ in., for dust removal

Detail C: Lower Guide Stop

Fence is two pieces of ¾-in. plywood glued together and surfaced with plastic laminate.

Cavity for bolt end

Locknut

Bolt, ⅜ in. dia., serves as stop.

½ in.

Block, ¾ in. thick with ⅜-in. T-nut, is glued to notch.

Notch, 1 in. x 13 in.

Top fence is 1⅝ in. above table.

Micro-Adjustable Tenon Jig

BY PAT WARNER

Most of the furniture making I do is experimental. Nothing in the design is standard. Consequently, when making tenons for joinery, I want a jig that will accommodate a wide range of sizes. Some adjustable woodworking jigs use the tap-and-clamp method. That works, but it's simply not very handy when you're making lots of different-sized tenons.

The jig I use to make tenons (see the photo at left and the top photo on p. 96) is nowhere near as sophisticated as some screw-driven woodworking machinery, but with a slight turn of the adjusting handle, I can dial in tenons to within 0.001 in. and cut 2-in.-long tenons in under a minute. The range of travel allows for shoulder widths up to ⅝ in. A straight bit in a router does the cutting. The jig works with either a template guide bushing or a bearing-guided pattern bit.

Although only one face is machined at a time, the work can be flipped, remounted, and milled in fewer than 10 seconds. The jig shown here will only cut two-faced tenons or four-faced tenons on narrow stock (approximately less than 1½ in.). For four-faced tenons on wider boards, you can (1) expand the size of the travel mechanism and clamp base to accommodate all four cuts; (2) cut the two short

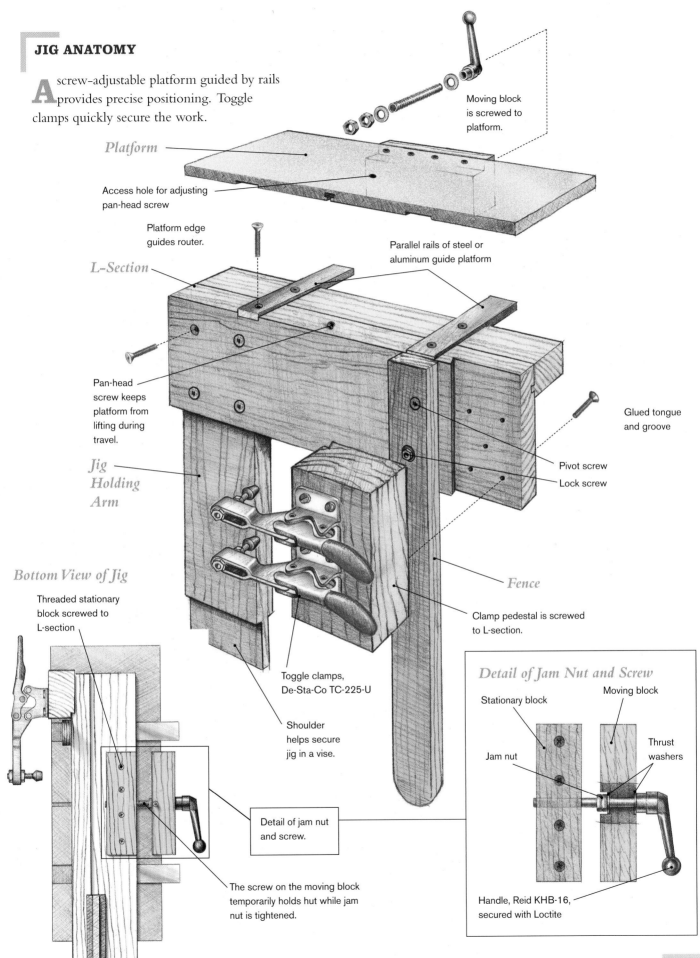

JIG ANATOMY

A screw-adjustable platform guided by rails provides precise positioning. Toggle clamps quickly secure the work.

Platform

Access hole for adjusting pan-head screw

Platform edge guides router.

Moving block is screwed to platform.

Parallel rails of steel or aluminum guide platform

L-Section

Pan-head screw keeps platform from lifting during travel.

Glued tongue and groove

Pivot screw

Lock screw

Jig Holding Arm

Fence

Clamp pedestal is screwed to L-section.

Bottom View of Jig

Threaded stationary block screwed to L-section

Toggle clamps, De-Sta-Co TC-225-U

Shoulder helps secure jig in a vise.

Detail of jam nut and screw.

The screw on the moving block temporarily holds nut while jam nut is tightened.

Detail of Jam Nut and Screw

Stationary block

Moving block

Jam nut

Thrust washers

Handle, Reid KHB-16, secured with Loctite

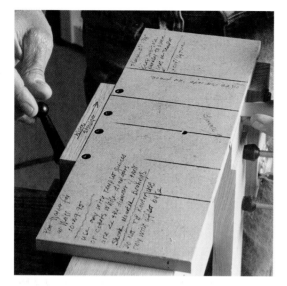

CUTTING A STACK OF TENONS IN UNDER THREE MINUTES. Precise adjustments and fast-acting toggle clamps on this jig allow you to make uniform router-cut tenons in quantity.

tenon faces by hand; or (3) build another similar jig for wider stock so that it will handle the other two faces.

Making the Jig

A simple L-section forms the backbone of this jig (see the drawings on the facing page). An adjustable platform above the work supports and guides the router, controlling the tenon size. This platform is positioned by a threaded rod (or lead screw) and held in alignment with metal guide rails. Toggle clamps secure the work in place, while a holding arm allows the jig to be secured in a vise or clamped to a bench. This jig will hold stock up to 8/4 thick and 10 in. wide and of any length.

The jig is made mostly of wood, but for many parts I used metal joinery methods, which produce rugged, accurate jigs. Rabbets or grooves align parts, and machine screws hold them together. I cut threads directly into the mating wooden part using machinist's taps. You could also use wood screws, carriage bolts, and threaded inserts for the assembly.

For strength, most of the wood used in this jig is red oak. The adjustable platform, however, is medium-density fiberboard (MDF) because I wanted a smooth, flat, stable material to guide the router.

L-Section and Guide Rails Begin by sizing the two pieces of stock that form the L-section. I joined these pieces with a shallow tongue and groove and glue. After the glue dries, router-cut all of the joinery and the guide-rail slots, and drill and countersink the holes for the machine screws.

I made the platform guide rails for this jig from ¼-in. by 1-in. steel flat bar. Alu-

minum flat bar would have worked just as well and been easier to cut and drill. The guide rails are let into and fastened to the L-section. The platform has mating slots to engage the rails. The four slots must be correctly spaced and parallel; otherwise, the platform will bind. I made a simple 10-in. by 17-in. rail template from ⅜-in.-thick MDF (see the photo below) to cut the slots. Using a top-bearing pattern bit, I cut two 1-in.-wide slots about 1 in. longer than the platform width and perpendicular to the open end (the reference edge) and slightly deeper than ⅛ in.

Cut the flat bar to length and drill and countersink the mounting-screw holes. Position the rails on the L-section and mark the center points for the screws. Be sure to set the rails back from the face of the L-section by about 1⁄16 in. to prevent a collision with the router bit later when you

A TEMPLATE MAKES MATCHED RAIL SLOTS. Align the front edge of the template with the L-section. Repeating this operation on the platform ensures that the rails stay in alignment and that the jig operates smoothly. The cuts are made with a top-bearing pattern bit.

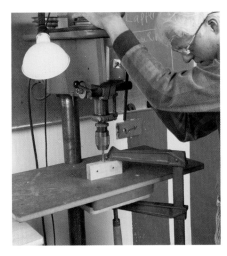

TAPPING HOLES. Turn the drill-press spindle by hand. Once the tap engages the wood block, it self-feeds, cutting uniform threads.

SQUARE THE FENCE TO THE PLATFORM. Tighten the two fence-mounting screws to lock the position. A slightly oversized hole allows the fence to be positioned at exactly 90°.

EDGE TRIMMING. Trim the platform edge parallel to the L-section face. The metal rails are set back from the face to prevent damaging the router. A vacuum hose catches the MDF dust.

trim the platform edge. Now, drill and tap these holes and mount the rails.

The Platform Once the rail slots have been milled, route a T-slot midway between the two rail slots. This T-slot engages a #10 pan-head sheet-metal screw in the L-section and keeps the platform from lifting during its travel. A hole through the platform allows convenient access to the pan-head screw for adjustment.

For the travel mechanism, I used a ⁵⁄₁₆-in., 18-tpi (threads per inch) screw thread. One full revolution produces ⅛ in. (0.056 in.) of platform travel; a quarter turn, therefore, produces 0.014 in. of platform travel, and so on.

The key parts of the travel mechanism are a threaded stationary block attached to the L-section, a moving block fastened to the platform, and a ⁵⁄₁₆-in., 18-tpi threaded rod with a lever. The moving block is rabbeted along the edge to join the platform and is drilled for a ⁵⁄₁₆-in. through-hole and counterbored on the inside face to house two nuts and a thrust washer. A thrust washer on the opposite side is recessed into a shallow counterbore. After screwing these two blocks in place, mark the pilot hole for

the thread through the ⁵⁄₁₆-in. hole in the moving block using a machinist's transfer punch. The transfer punch has the same nominal shank diameter as the drill. A small point exactly in the center of the punch perfectly centers the two holes. Now remove the stationary block and cut threads using a drill press (unpowered) as a tapping fixture (see the top left photo on p. 77).

Two nuts tightened against each other hold the screw and the lever assembly in the moving block. The pan-head screw is tightened against the innermost nut to prevent it from turning while the jam nut is tightened. Once the nuts are tight, the pan-head screw is backed away, allowing the shaft to turn freely.

The Fence, Clamp Pedestal and Jig Holding Arm Cut the stock for the fence. The fence pivots on a ⁵⁄₁₆-in., 18-tpi flat-head machine screw. The lower screw has an elongated hole, which allows the fence to be positioned exactly 90° to the under-side of the platform (see the center photo above).

Sources

Toggle clamps and handle

Reid Tool Supply Co.®
2265 Black Creek Rd.
Muskegon, MI 49444
(800) 253-0421
Also available at local industrial supply houses and through other mail-order hardware suppliers.

Thread-locking adhesive
Loctite® is sold in most automotive-supply stores.

To mount the clamp pedestal, transfer the bolt-hole pattern from the L-section. Use the clamp base as a pattern to locate the pilot holes for the mounting screws. The jig holding arm is lap-bolted to the L-section. Transfer the mounting-screw location from the L-section. The shoulders on the end of the arm help keep it square in the vise and resist rotation during use.

Truing Up the Platform Edge Remove the fence and clamp pedestal and secure the jig in a vise. Now, extend about ½ in. of platform past the face of the L-section. Using a router with a flush-trimming bit (bearing on the end of the bit), cut the platform edge parallel to the L-section face (see the top right photo on p. 97). This matches the platform edge to the L-section face. Reassemble the jig, and you're ready to make tenons.

Making Tenons with the Jig

I prefer using a fixed-base router when I make tenons with this jig. A plunge router

DIALING IN THE PERFECT TENON. If the test cut results in too big a tenon, adjust the jig and cut again. The author has made a number of jigs based on the same basic design; the screw clamps on the jig shown here will hold wider stock than the jig shown in the top photo on p. 96. The top surface of the platform is a handy place for notes and reference lines for cutting multiples or to repeat a setup at a later time.

may be better for multiple-depth cuts, but it's difficult to plunge one safely along an edge because of the small footprint and high center of gravity.

Install the cutter and guide collar on your router, and set the depth of cut. Adjust the toggle clamps to the stock thickness. Very large work may require the addition of a C-clamp. Be sure to position the work against both the fence and the underside of the platform. Routing in this orientation, across the grain, quickly peels away material. Nevertheless, deep cuts should be done in multiple passes.

Position the platform at your best first guess and rout the first cheek of the tenon. I usually climb-cut (moving along the edge right to left) because there is so little resistance to the cut. When climb cutting, take light cuts to avoid a runaway router. Reposition the work and cut the opposite cheek without moving the platform. Test the tenon in its mortise. If it's too big, determine by how much and divide by two. Then move the platform back by that amount and repeat the cut (see the photo at left).

PAT WARNER is a woodworker and college instructor who lives in Escondido, California.

Shop-Built Horizontal Mortiser

My wife and I had just transformed our basement into a sitting area, home office, alcove, and bar, but it was clear to me that we weren't finished. I envisioned three major furniture projects I'd have to complete. We needed a built-in storage cabinet in the sitting area for a television and VCR; base cabinets in the office for a computer, a printer, a copier, and a fax machine; and shelf units in the alcove for books, albums, and assorted art objects. I planned to build the shelf units in a Craftsman style, based on some bookcases I'd seen in an article by C. Michael Vogt in *Fine Woodworking.* I could foresee dozens—if not hundreds—of mortise-and-tenon joints, and I began to question my plan to tackle all of these projects.

I had read an article about mortise-and-loose-tenon joints, and I remembered that loose tenons are simple to make. If I could speed up the mortising process, I could complete my three projects in a reasonable

BY JOHN F. MATOUSEK

Using a router and two sliding tables, this homemade setup is a versatile joint-making machine.

One Nifty Shop-Built Machine

The author designed this setup primarily as a router-based mortiser. By being able to adjust the cutting edge in relation to the workpiece in three dimensions—up and down, in and out, side to side—he ended up with a rig that is as easy to use as it is accurate. By bolting the top table to the back panel that holds the router, he also uses it for other tasks, such as shaping the edges of raised panels.

Router base pivots up and down.

Flattened ½-in.-dia. dowel stiffens table.

Adjustable stops register workpiece.

Hold-down bar secures workpiece.

Top table moves side to side.

Bolts with wing nuts lock router base in position. Adjustable stops limit side-to-side movement of top table.

Flattened ½-in. dia. dowel stiffens table.

Hose connector for dust collection

Tables ride on ball-bearing drawer slides.

Bottom table moves in and out.

HOW IT WORKS

The first cut for a mortise begins by plunging the workpiece into a spinning router bit.

The remaining mortise emerges by moving the workpiece left to right in relation to the bit.

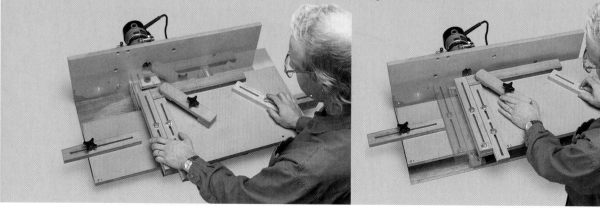

amount of time. So I began to design a machine to make mortises.

The Machine Is Designed to Make Accurate Cuts

I wanted a system that could be set up easily and be operated safely and that could accurately duplicate a mortising operation. Also, I needed a machine that could raise or lower the cutting bit as necessary for precise adjustments. But I wasn't sure that my scheme would work, and I didn't want to spend a lot of money on a failed experiment, so I built this setup with scraps and hardware left over from previous projects. The design I finally built (see the drawing on the facing page) was that of a horizontal compound-mortising table. As designed, it is meant to mortise mostly ¾-in.-thick lumber workpieces, using a solid-carbide, ¼-in. spiral upcut bit, powered by a standard 1½-hp router, which I mounted on a vertical back panel. (I did buy a new Porter-Cable model No. 690 router, figuring that I could use it in the shop even if my experiment failed.)

The machine has two movable tables. The top table moves at right angles to the bit, and the bottom table moves parallel to it. I mounted two drawer slides (Accuride model No. C-1029 center-mount slides) under the tables to provide for the side-to-side and front-to-back movements of the tables. Movable stops at each end of the bottom table can be set to control the distance the top table can move and thus the length of the mortise.

Indexed Adjustments Are the Key to Accuracy
To improve accuracy and to speed up the mortising process, I wanted stops wherever possible to position the workpiece for mortising rather than to depend upon pencil layout lines. By butting the workpiece against a stop, I could ensure the accuracy and the reliability of matching stile-and-rail joints.

ONE TURN OF THE THREADED BOLT CAN RAISE OR LOWER THE ROUTER. The author rigged up the adjusting device shown here to enhance his ability to fine-tune the height of the router bit in relation to the workpiece. The router swivels up and down on a Plexiglas base that is hinged on one end of the vertical panel to which it is secured.

For a given frame or set of frames, I wanted to position the stops only one time for both left and right mortises. The other option would have been to reposition the stops when going from a left to a right mortise, but it would be faster to flip the workpiece over, end for end.

To position the mortise with such a high level of precision in the center of the workpiece, the router would have to be mounted on the back panel so that it could be raised or lowered until the bit cut into the exact center of the workpiece. Using a threaded bolt to raise and lower the router (see the photo above) and a dial indicator to check the adjustments, I could fine-tune the height of the cutting bit very easily.

To make a mortise near the middle of a stile—such as that required for a center rail—the stops have to be removed, and you must use layout lines to position the workpiece for the cut.

The Original Setup Needed Some Tweaking

The prototype of this machine worked beyond my expectations, except for one defect. When moving the top table forward into the cutting bit, I tended to press down on the table with enough force to deflect it sufficiently that it cut the mortise off center. To correct this, I snugly fitted a flattened ½-in. dowel to the underside of each end of the top table and added a little wax on the surfaces where the dowels slid against the bottom table.

Also, I added a hold-down bar on the top table for safety and to improve the accuracy of each setup. And finally, a 1¼-in.-dia. vacuum hose (mounted directly beneath the router bit and connected to a standard shop vacuum) collects most of the dust and chips generated by mortising operations.

Use This Machine as a Mortiser or as a Conventional Router Table

After setting up the machine to cut a mortise, it's best to plunge the workpiece repeatedly into the cutting bit, drilling a series of holes, by moving the bottom table in and out and adjusting the top table a little for each plunge.

After that, clean up the sidewalls of the mortise by moving the top table left to right between the stops (which are mounted on both sides of the bottom table). Also, by clamping a fence on the top table 45° to the back panel, you can drill mortises into the ends of a 45° miter using essentially the same procedure.

By bolting the top table to the back panel—using two brackets on the underside—you can turn this machine into a router

table, good for any number of shaping tasks. For years I've wanted to cut raised panels, but I've always felt uneasy about using either a 4½-in.-dia. shaper cutter or a vertical router table. The amount of spinning steel in a large cutter scares me, and using a vertical panel-raising bit in a vertical router doesn't appeal to me because it's awkward to move a large panel through the cutter resting only on its edge. But by using a vertical panel-raising bit horizontally in this machine, I was able to address all of my concerns and to get good results because the panel lies flat on the table, and it's easy to control.

Loose Tenons can be Made in Large Quantities

I manufacture a variety of loose tenons before I need them, making 100 or so at a time in varying widths and lengths. I use ¼-in. hardboard, ripped to width, and I round over the edges with a ¼-in. bullnose bit. Because the length of the mortise can be controlled with considerable accuracy by the mortising machine, the width of the tenons is not a critical dimension, and I'm able to stockpile a pretty good supply without worrying about whether they will fit later on.

I completed my three projects in a reasonable period of time and in the process made several hundred mortise-and-loose-tenon joints with safety, accuracy and speed. This machine is quite specialized, and I don't have to use it very often; but when I do, it saves me a bundle of time.

JOHN F. MATOUSEK lives in Englewood, Colorado, and is retired from his career as an information systems engineer.

Micro-Adjustable Router Fence

BY PAT WARNER

To get on with the business of table routing, you need a stand, a flat router-table top, and an adjustable fence. The stand and top do nothing but support the work. The fence, on the other hand, is the key to precision and efficiency. The fence is almost always in play and needs constant adjustment to handle the router table's ever-changing responsibilities.

As my hair whitens, I look for less frustrating and more efficient ways of spending my time. My fence did not result from an accident or a guess but from a lot of experimentation and testing. It is a precision joiner's fence that can be made for around $80, and it should save

you countless hours of shop time for years to come. The fence can handle bits up to 2⅜ in. dia. but can't handle the largest bits, such as panel-raisers. You can position the fence solidly and lock it anywhere in its travel in 5 seconds or 10 seconds, and it can be adjusted by thousandths of an inch.

Once you index the bit to the edge of your workpiece, the cutting depth can be set quickly and precisely. The micro-

DON'T GET HUNG UP ON THIS FENCE

It's not as complicated as it looks. There are only four main parts: A base that attaches to your router table; a carrier that slides back and forth on the base and carries the fence halves; the stiffeners; and the fence faces that make up the two fence halves. In use, the parts are screwed and clamped to each other to form a solid assembly. The other stuff, the micro-adjustment components and the dial indicator, just hitch a ride on this basic unit.

Note: Except for the four clamp levers, which thread into Propell T-nuts, all screws on this jig thread into tapped holes in wood.

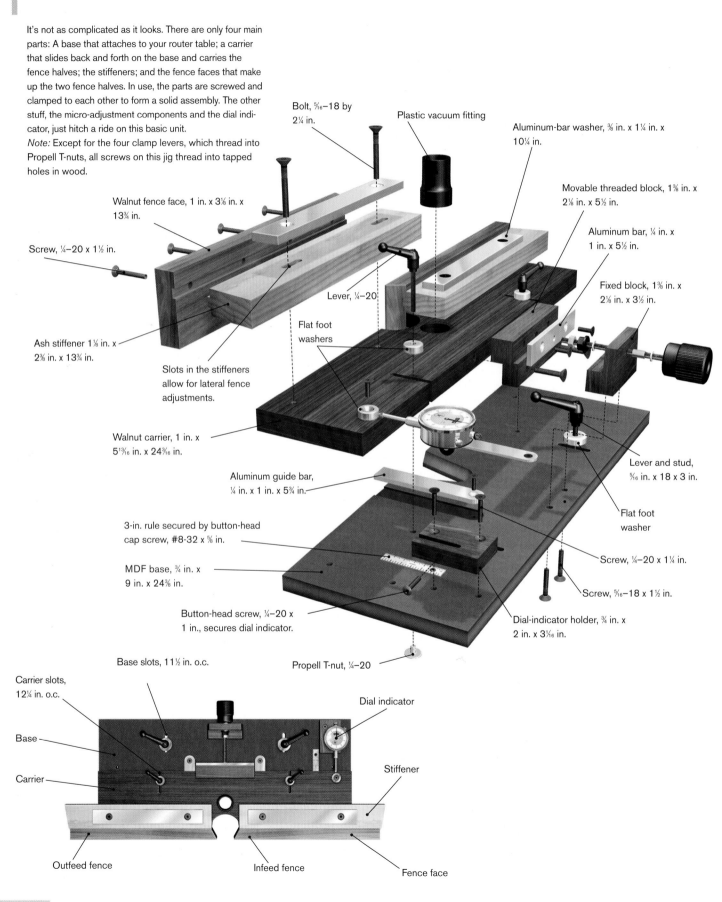

Bolt, ⁵⁄₁₆–18 by 2¼ in.

Plastic vacuum fitting

Aluminum-bar washer, ⅜ in. x 1¼ in. x 10¼ in.

Walnut fence face, 1 in. x 3⅛ in. x 13¾ in.

Movable threaded block, 1⅜ in. x 2⅛ in. x 5½ in.

Aluminum bar, ¼ in. x 1 in. x 5½ in.

Screw, ¼–20 x 1½ in.

Lever, ¼–20

Fixed block, 1⅜ in. x 2⅛ in. x 3½ in.

Ash stiffener 1⅛ in. x 2⅜ in. x 13¾ in.

Flat foot washers

Slots in the stiffeners allow for lateral fence adjustments.

Walnut carrier, 1 in. x 5¹³⁄₁₆ in. x 24³⁄₁₆ in.

Aluminum guide bar, ¼ in. x 1 in. x 5¾ in.

Lever and stud, ⁵⁄₁₆ x 18 x 3 in.

Flat foot washer

3-in. rule secured by button-head cap screw, #8-32 x ⅝ in.

MDF base, ¾ in. x 9 in. x 24⅝ in.

Screw, ¼–20 x 1¼ in.

Screw, ⁵⁄₁₆–18 x 1½ in.

Button-head screw, ¼–20 x 1 in., secures dial indicator.

Dial-indicator holder, ¾ in. x 2 in. x 3¹⁄₁₆ in.

Base slots, 11½ in. o.c.

Propell T-nut, ¼–20

Carrier slots, 12¼ in. o.c.

Dial indicator

Base

Carrier

Stiffener

Outfeed fence

Infeed fence

Fence face

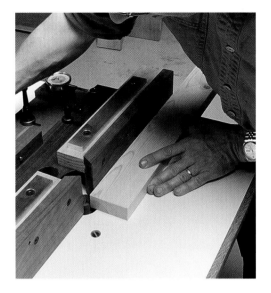

THIS PRECISION ROUTER FENCE ATTACHES TO YOUR ROUTER TABLE. **A micro-adjustment screw and a dial indicator let you creep up on the perfect joint. The outfeed fence can be shimmed out for edge jointing.**

adjustment mechanism allows you to make slight changes in a rabbet, dado, mortise, or other joint while sneaking up on a tight fit. For material-hogging bits, successive passes can be made in precise increments. And climb-cutting (to prevent tearout) is safer because a very light cut is easy to produce.

The fence moves in a straight line on two ¼-in. by 1-in. aluminum guide bars and is micro-adjusted accurately along the dial indicator's 1 in. of travel. The fence's travel is also monitored with a 3-in. Starrett rule. Two small clamp levers lock the micro-adjustment section of the fence.

The base is slotted for larger clamp levers that screw into T-nuts under a router-table top. These slots allow for another 1⅜ in. of rough adjustment. A second set of T-nuts in the table will double the amount of rough adjustment.

The fence creates a vacuum funnel to collect sawdust. And the outfeed fence can be shimmed out for edge-jointing.

Making the Fence

This is not a particularly difficult piece to make, but you must assemble this fence in

Routing the Matching Dadoes

A template ensures accuracy. A ¾-in. MDF template makes it easy to rout the matching shallow dadoes (1). To rout the stopped dadoes in the base, center the template along the front edge of the base and clamp it. Use a top-bearing-guided (or pattern maker's) bit to cut the shallow dadoes. Do the same thing in the walnut carrier (2). This time, however, the dadoes run completely across this narrower component. Make these dadoes a bit deeper than ⅛ in. for clearance. With the aluminum guide bars in place, the carrier and base should fit together and slide easily (3).

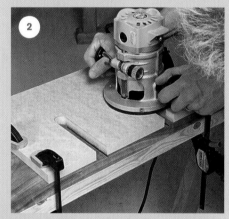

Position the Fence Halves

Allow room for adjustment. With the fence faces about 1 in. apart, butt the outfeed fence against the carrier and transfer-punch through the outer side of each slot in the stiffener to locate the tapped holes below (1). Note that the outfeed slots are wider to allow this side to be offset for edge jointing. Do the same with the infeed fence, but shim it out from the carrier 0.006 in. to 0.008 in. first, to allow room for slight adjustment later (2). A folded dollar bill makes the perfect shim at each end. Drill the tapped holes in the carrier, cut and drill the aluminum-bar washers, and fasten the fence halves in place (3).

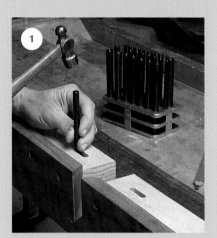

a specific order, or you'll be starting over. If it's any consolation, my first one was less than perfect. I recommend buying one set of hardware but enough of the less-expensive materials to allow for two attempts. This fence assembly has four main components: the base, the carrier, the fence faces and the fence stiffeners. Add the micro-adjustment system and the dial indicator, and you are basically there.

Begin with the MDF Base Use a router or bandsaw to cut out the V-shaped cutter/vacuum path in the medium-density-fiberboard (MDF) base. Bevel the walls of this channel 60° to facilitate chip extraction.

Plunge-rout the two slots for the clamp levers. Next come the shallow dadoes that will hold the aluminum guide bars. Use your router table to make the template for these 1-in.-wide by ⅛-in.-deep dadoes. To create parallel dadoes, run the same side of the template against the fence each time.

Center the template along the length of the base and line it up with the edge. Use a bearing-guided bit to cut the dadoes. Drill the two holes for the fixed end of the micro-adjustment assembly. The rest of the holes in this base will be located from the components you'll make next.

Use a Straight-Grained Piece of Walnut for the Carrier I chose walnut for the carrier because the wood is relatively stable and can be resurfaced easily.

Rout two matching dadoes with the same template you used on the base. For clearance, cut them 0.005 in. to 0.010 in. deeper than the dadoes in the base. Next cut the two stopped slots into the back of the carrier for the small clamp levers, spaced 12¼ in. on center. Drill the 1½-in. hole for the vacuum port (on the centerline, 2⁵⁄₁₆ in. from the front edge). Now cut the deep semicircle into the front edge, where the cutter will reside. For a better chip pathway to the vacuum port, relieve the underside with a ⅜-in. cove cutter. Finally, cut the stopped dado for the Starrett rule. I have seen the widths of these rules vary by up to ¹⁄₆₄ in., so match the dado width to your own rule.

Fence Faces Are Screwed to the Stiffeners I used 1-in.-thick walnut for the fence faces, more for the wood's stability than for its durability. It's a good idea to make some spares because these parts will wear out. Cut a 60° bevel on the ends that will be near the router bit. Drill and countersink them for the ¼-20 screws. Cut a groove in the back of each fence face (⁷⁄₁₆ in. wide by ³⁄₁₆ in. deep) centered along the screw-hole line. These grooves will mate with tongues in the ash stiffeners, locating the fence faces just off the surface of your router table, to allow for sawdust clearance.

The stiffeners can be cut 12 in. long to square off with the end of the fence faces, but I make them longer than the faces for decorative purposes. Plunge-rout the two ⅜-in.-wide stopped slots in the outfeed stiffener. Cut ⁵⁄₁₆-in.-wide slots in the infeed stiffener. Screws will pass through the aluminum-bar washers and these slots to hold the two fence halves to the carrier. The outfeed slots are wider to allow the outfeed side to be shimmed out approximately ½ in. for edge jointing.

Next, machine centered tongues to fit the grooves in the fence faces. Make them a tight fit. For chip clearance, position the height of the tongues so that the bottoms of the fence faces will be just above the surface of your router table. Fit the faces to the stiffeners and transfer the centers of the holes in the faces through to the stiffeners. A transfer punch does this job more precisely than any improvised solution, such as a brad-point drill, and a cheap set of

punches will make a handy addition to your shop. Drill the ¹³⁄₆₄-in. pilot holes in the tongues of the stiffeners and tap them for the ¼-20 screws. Screw together the fence faces and stiffeners.

Position the Infeed and Outfeed Fences Center the assembled fence parts, 1 in. apart, on the front of the carrier. Butt the outfeed fence against the carrier and clamp it down. Shim the infeed fence 0.006 in. to 0.008 in. away from the carrier and clamp it (a dollar bill makes a handy 0.004-in.-thick shim). The extra play will make it easier to align the infeed side with the outfeed side. I put ⅜-in. and ⁵⁄₁₆-in. transfer punches through the respective slots in the stiffeners to locate the tapped holes in the carrier. Transfer the centers through the outside ends of all four slots, to allow each half to be slid outward for larger router bits when you use the fence. Remove the fence halves, and drill and tap the carrier.

Assemble the Micro-Adjustment System The micro-adjustment assembly consists of a fixed hardwood block with a bearing in it and a movable hardwood block faced with a bar of aluminum for more thread purchase. Any chunk of steel or aluminum will suffice; for the blocks I used jatoba, but any hardwood will work. The aluminum bar is bolted to a rabbet in the movable block, but the threaded hole will be located later, after the fence has been assembled. Center and fasten this block to the carrier. Now fasten the fixed block to the base.

Attach the Dial Indicator The dial indicator for this fence measures 1 in. of travel. The indicator is attached to a hardwood block, which serves as a holder. Form a slot in the block for the bracket on the rear of this particular indicator. Drill a ¹³⁄₆₄-in. hole

Add the Rule, the Dial, and the Micro-Adjustment Assembly

SLIDE THE RULE INTO THE SLOT IN THE CARRIER UP TO ITS 1-IN. MARK. Use the hole you drilled in the rule to lay out the tapped hole in the base.

ALIGN THE DIAL INDICATOR WITH ITS STOP ON THE CARRIER. Push the unit forward until 0.020 in. to 0.040 in. of travel is left. Transfer its holes with a center punch and drill and tap the base.

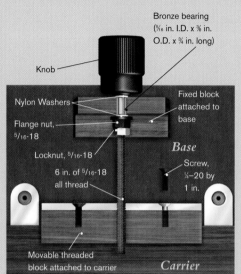

MICRO-ADJUSTABLE ASSEMBLY

The knob-and-spindle assembly runs through a bronze bearing in the fixed block and screws into the threads that are tapped into the aluminum and wood of the movable block.

LOCATE THE MICRO-ADJUSTMENT ASSEMBLY. Transfer the hole in the fixed block on the base to the movable block on the carrier. Drill and tap the movable block.

---

through the slot for the ¼-20 by 1-in. button-head screw. Tap 1 in. of threads, then bore out the thinner side of the slot to ¼ in. for clearance. Drill and countersink the block in two places so that you can fasten it to the base. Locate the rule and the dial indicator after the assembly has been completed. The stop for the plunger is a thick machined washer. Drill and tap for its cap screw and attach it.

Finishing Up

Transfer the centers of the ⁵⁄₁₆-in. fence bolt holes in the carrier to the aluminum-bar washers, centering each bar over its pair of

bolt holes. Drill and countersink ²¹⁄₆₄-in. holes in the aluminum. Now assemble and fasten the fence halves to the carrier.

Round the ends of the aluminum guide bars to fit the stopped ends of the slots in the base, as I do, or leave the ends square and square off the end of each slot. Drill and countersink the guides for the machine screws that fasten them to the base. Drill and tap the base for these screws and attach the guide bars.

Now drop the fence assembly onto the guide bars and slide the backs of the fences against the base. Use the ends of the slots in the walnut carrier to mark the holes in the base for the two T-nut inserts. The smaller lever clamps will reside in these slots. Remove the fence assembly and drill small holes through the base to the bottom side for location. Flip the base, and drill and counterbore the bottom for the T-nuts.

Reattach the fence assembly to the base, again butting the fence faces against the base. Insert the small clamp levers and lock down the assembly. You can now locate the holes for both the Starrett rule and the dial-indicator holder.

Drill a ⁵⁄₃₂-in. hole in the Starrett rule on the first ½-in. mark. You'll need carbide to get through the tempered steel. Slide the rule under the carrier to the 1-in. mark and locate the hole for the button-head screw. If you don't have a ⁵⁄₃₂-in. carbide bit, you can hold down the rule with double-faced tape.

With the dial indicator fastened to its holder, locate the unit so that the indicator's plunger is centered on the stop (you attached it earlier) and only 0.020 in. to 0.040 in. of travel is left in the indicator. Transfer the holes in the holder to the base and drill and tap the base for the rule and the dial indicator.

With the fence reassembled, insert the bronze bearing in the fixed block and transfer its center through to the aluminum bar in the movable block. Drill (¼ in.) and tap the movable block for the adjustment screw.

Screw the knob onto its threaded rod with a drop of Loctite or other glue to hold it in place. Insert the knob screw through the fixed block with a nylon washer on both sides. Spin down the flange nut and locknut; allow no slop. With the carrier riding on its guides, thread the screw into the movable block. Drive the fence all the way to the 1-in. mark on the rule and lock it down. Last, press-fit the plastic vacuum fitting into its 1½-in. opening.

To attach the entire assembly to your router table, center the fence opening on your router table and clamp down the base. Locate and drill the holes in the tabletop for the larger T-nuts, which are for the larger set of clamp levers.

Using the Fence

To get up and routing, lock the base to your router table, attach your vacuum hose and insert your chosen cutter.

Loosen the aluminum-bar washers and align the fence halves with a long straight-edge, moving their inside edges close to your router bit. Then tighten down each side.

Release the smaller clamp levers for micro-adjustments and lock them down before cutting. Make some test cuts. If the fences aren't exactly perpendicular to your tabletop, square them up by placing paper shims under the stiffeners.

There are few frills on this tool. All components work together, with clamps and washers designed to flatten the parts and create a stable assembly. The drive mechanism is relatively inexpensive, and you can save another $30 if you decide to omit the dial indicator and 3-in. rule.

PAT WARNER is a woodworker and college instructor who lives in Escondido, California. John White, *Fine Woodworking's* shop manager, helped with this article.

Sources

Reid Tool Supply
800-253-0421
Clamp levers, knob, dial indicator and other assorted hardware

Bruss Fasteners
800-536-0009
Propell T-nuts

DeWalt
800-433-9258
Plastic vacuum fitting (1 1/2 in.), part No. 328592-00

L.S. Starrett®
978-249-3551
3-in. Starrett rule, part No. C604R-3
A complete parts list, with all Reid part numbers, is available on our Web site: www. finewoodworking.com

No-Frills Router Table

BY GARY ROGOWSKI

Remember the commercial about the knife that sliced, diced, and performed myriad other tasks, even gliding through a tomato after cutting a metal pipe? Well, that's what a router table is like. You can cut stopped and through grooves, dadoes, rabbets, and dovetailed slots. You can raise panels and cut sliding dovetails, tenons and mortises. It's no won-der that many woodworkers can't imagine working wood without one.

But router tables can be expensive. In one woodworking catalog, I saw a number of packages selling for between $250 and $300. I'd rather spend my money on wood. That same money would buy some really spectacular fiddleback Oregon walnut.

I've been building furniture for years, and my bare-bones router table has given me excellent, accurate results. The router table in the photo on the facing page is a variation that is inexpensive, easy to construct, and extremely versatile. It's a simple, three-sided box made from a half-sheet of ¾-in.-thick melamine with the front left open for easy access to the router. I made mine with a top that's 24 in. deep by 32 in. wide, which keeps it light enough to move around yet big enough to handle about anything I'd use a router table for. It's 16 in. high, which is a good height for placing it on boards on sawhorses or on a low assembly bench.

Biscuits and Dadoes Join Parts

When you buy the melamine, make sure the sheet is flat. And buy it in a color other than blinding white, which is tough on the eyes.

The melamine I used had a particleboard core. Biscuits are stronger than screws in particleboard, so I joined the two sides to the top with #20 biscuits. To make the cuts in the underside of the top, I took a spacer block 5 in. wide, aligned it with the end of the top, and set my plate joiner against it for the cuts. The width of the block determined the overhang of the top. Marks on the spacer block gave me my centers.

The biscuit joints probably would have been plenty strong by themselves, but I wanted to add a little extra strength to the joint. So I decided to dado the underside of the top for the sides. I couldn't dado very deeply, though, or the biscuits would have bottomed out. I settled on a ¹⁄₁₆-in.-deep pass centered over the biscuit slots (see the top photo at right). Before cutting the dado, however, I dry-fitted the sides and top with biscuits in place to check the alignment. Then I scored heavily around the

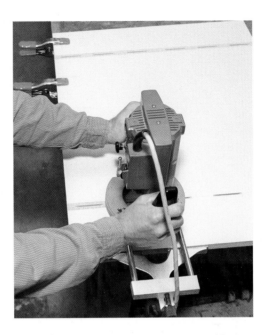

SHALLOW DADO INCREASES GLUE SURFACE. To strengthen the joints between the sides and top, the author routs a dado ¹⁄₁₆ in. deep in the underside of the top directly over biscuit slots.

FIBERBOARD BACK PREVENTS RACKING. Although it's only ¼ in. thick, the fiberboard back greatly strengthens the table. The fiberboard is glued and screwed into a rabbet all around the back of the table.

edges of the side pieces with a marking knife and routed the shallow dadoes.

Before gluing the sides to the top, I rabbeted the back edge of the two sides for a ¼-in. panel to strengthen the table and prevent it from racking. Then I glued the sides to the top one at a time, using battens to distribute the clamping pressure. I made sure each side was square to the top and waited for the glue to set up.

CUT THE HOLE WITH A ROUTER BIT. With the router base screwed to the underside of the top, the author advances his largest bit through the table. Go slowly.

I used a router and rabbeting bit to cut a stopped rabbet in the back edge of the top. Then I glued and screwed down the ¼-in. medium-density fiberboard (MDF) back panel (see the bottom photo above). Hardboard or plywood would have worked as well.

I use a fixed-base router in my router table because it's lighter than most plunge routers and won't cause the table to sag over time. Also, it's much easier to change bits. I just drop the router motor out of the base, change bits, reinstall the router and I'm back to work.

I attached the router base to the underside of the tabletop with machine screws that go down through the top into the tapped holes in the router base. To mark the location of the screw holes, I removed the router subbase and made pencil marks on the top. Then I drilled and countersunk holes into the tabletop.

With the base attached to the table, I marked out where the bit hole should go and drilled a ¾-in. hole into the table. I put a 2⅛-in.-dia. chamfer bit in my router—the largest bit I have. I started the tool and gradually moved the bit up and through the tabletop (see the left photo above).

To prevent workpieces from diving into this hole when using small bits, I made a set of inserts that fit in a shallow recess around the bit hole. Holes in the inserts accommodate bits of different sizes with minimal clearance. I routed out the rabbeted recesses for the inserts first, using a plunge router guided by a straightedge. I squared the corners with a chisel.

I made the inserts of ¼-in. tempered hardboard. Their square shape keeps them from spinning during use and makes them easy to fit. I cut a bunch of them on the table saw and then sanded each to a perfect fit on a belt sander.

L-Shaped Fence Provides Dust Collection

The fence I've always used might be called low-tech, but there's really no tech to it at all. It's simply a straight, wide, flat piece of wood jointed so that one edge is square to a face. I clamp it to the router table wherever I need it. The fence doesn't have to be parallel to a table edge to work. When a bit needs to be partially hidden for a cut, I use another board with a recess cut into its face.

The only thing my primitive fence lacks is dust collection. Hooking up a vacuum or

CLAMP THE FENCE SQUARE. **Adjust the clamps to get the two pieces square over the entire length of the fence.**

a dust collector just won't work in some situations, such as when I plow a groove. But with other operations—raising a panel, rabbeting a drawer or box bottom, or cutting an edge profile—having a fence with a dust port can really help clear the air.

The fence I built for this router table is made of two pieces of ¾-in.-thick MDF about 4½ in. wide and 49 in. long rabbeted together to form an L-shape (see the right photo on p. 114). I cut a semi-circular hole at the center of each for dust collection. This allows for better pickup. I also routed slots in the vertical part of the fence so I could attach auxiliary fences for specific operations, such as raising panels or rabbeting. Once these slots are routed, the two pieces of the fence can be glued together. Make sure the fence clamps up square because virtually everything you use the table for depends on it.

To create sidewalls for the dust-collection hook-up, I added two triangular-shaped pieces of ¾-in.-thick MDF to frame the dust-collection port (see the right photo on p. 114). I glued these triangles in place on either side of the dust holes, just rubbing them in place and letting them set up without clamping. After the glue had cured, I filed the triangles flush with the fence, top and bottom.

To complete the dust-collection hook-up, I measured the diameter of the nozzle on my shop vacuum and cut a hole to accommodate it in a piece of ¼-in. hardboard. I left the hardboard oversized, clamped it to the drill-press table and used a circle cutter on my drill press. Then I cut the hardboard to size and glued and screwed it to the two triangular walls.

Auxiliary Fences Solve Specific Problems

A two-piece auxiliary fence can be used to close up the area around the bit when routing profiles, rabbeting, or performing similar operations. This way, there's no chance of a small piece diving into the gap between bit and fence. And with a smaller opening around the bit, the dust collector or vacuum will work more efficiently. When the fence is situated back from the bit, such as when mortising, another set of auxiliary pieces can be used, so there's no gap between the two halves (see the left photo on p. 114).

I made the auxiliary fence from two more pieces of MDF. The auxiliary fence is drilled and countersunk for machine screws that ride in slots cut in the main fence. I use nuts and washers to tighten the two pieces in position.

When using the auxiliary fence, I close the two halves around the moving bit to provide a custom fence. When I'm done with it, I can set the fence aside for future use or just cut it off square and use it again. Closing the fence into a bit with a diameter that's less than the thickness of the fence

USING A CLOSED AUXILIARY FENCE. Routing away from the fence calls for auxiliary pieces butted tightly together to form a smooth, continuous surface.

SCREW DUST-COLLECTION PORT TO FENCE. Smear a bead of glue along the two triangular sidewalls. Drill holes and screw the hardboard back to them.

will not open up the back of the fence to the dust-collection port. In this situation, I pivot the fence through the spinning bit before setting the fence for depth of cut.

Make sure that the outfeed side of the fence doesn't stick out any farther than the infeed side. If it does, it will prevent you from feeding your work smoothly past the bit. If your work catches on the outfeed side of the fence, easing its leading edge with a file or a chisel may help. If it doesn't, you can always shim the infeed side with slips of paper.

Another router table problem I've found is what to do with large upright pieces, such as panels cut with a vertical panel-

raising bit. The solution is to screw a taller auxiliary fence to the main fence. The fence can be pivoted right into the bit, so there's no gap on either the infeed or outfeed side of the bit, yet there's dust collection behind the bit.

GARY ROGOWSKI has been building furniture in Portland, Oregon, since 1974 and teaching woodworking since 1980. He is a contributing editor to *Fine Woodworking.*

Get the Most from Your Router Table

BY PAT WARNER

Judging from the growing ranks of ready-made router tables and the numerous articles in magazines on how to build one, the router table has become a must-have tool for woodworkers. Unfortunately, instruction in the correct use of this tool has been all but ignored. I can tell from the e-mails I receive that too many woodworkers are using risky methods to obtain disappointing results.

Most routing can be done safely and accurately on the router table if certain guidelines are followed. Here I'll cover three keys to success and talk about bits. I'll also discuss which routers are okay for use in a table and how to determine the correct feed rate. And I'll give a few tips on getting smooth cuts every time, even with special cuts or bits.

Three Keys to Successful Routing

If you decide to build your own router table, you are welcome to make it as sophisticated as possible. However, the table does not have to be that complex. All that is required for maximum control of the workpiece and highest quality of cut are a flat table that's at a comfortable working height and a good fence.

Table-Routing Technique

Stance

Standing to the right-hand side of the router table allows you to feed a longer board with fewer hand movements.

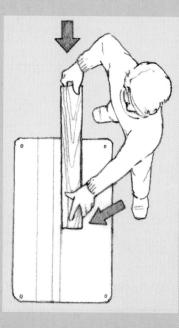

Hand Position

The left hand guides the stock as the right hand pushes. Let the workpiece slip through the fingers of the left hand. Maintain steady forward momentum with the right hand.

END-GRAIN SLED

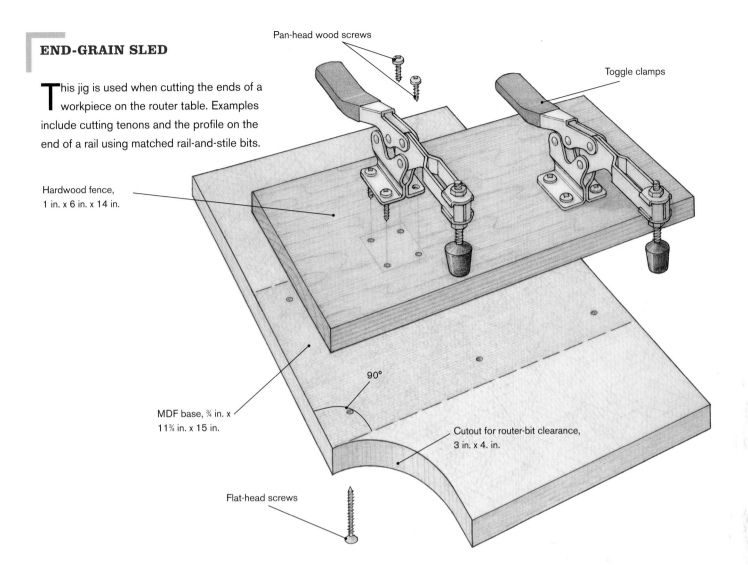

This jig is used when cutting the ends of a workpiece on the router table. Examples include cutting tenons and the profile on the end of a rail using matched rail-and-stile bits.

Pan-head wood screws

Toggle clamps

Hardwood fence,
1 in. x 6 in. x 14 in.

90°

MDF base, ¾ in. x
11¾ in. x 15 in.

Cutout for router-bit clearance,
3 in. x 4. in.

Flat-head screws

If the work is not at a comfortable height, any form of routing will be a struggle. Even for shorter woodworkers, the standard bench height (34 in. to 36 in.) is too low for routing. You can't see the work, and if you try, you'll fold yourself in half. What level feels comfortable varies considerably even among those of the same height. A good way to discover what feels right for you is to use a drill-press table as your experimental height platform. Hold a workpiece as if you were routing it, and adjust the table to see what height feels comfortable.

Whether a router tabletop has been "windowed" for an insert or not, it must be flat and uninterrupted. If the workpiece bumps into any minor changes of height

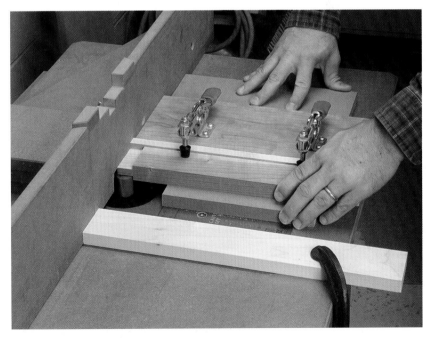

CUTTING TENONS. This rail and a backing block are secured against the sled by two toggle clamps. A stop block prevents cutting into the jig.

LONG-GRAIN SLED

This jig is used for running the long side of a workpiece past the cutter. The sled can help out the long edges of rails and stiles using one cutter from a matched set. It can also aid in cutting decorative profiles and moldings.

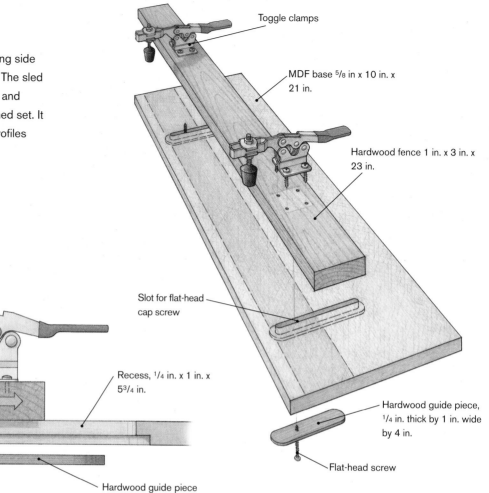

Toggle clamps

MDF base ⅝ in x 10 in. x 21 in.

Hardwood fence 1 in. x 3 in. x 23 in.

Slot for flat-head cap screw

Hardwood guide piece, ¼ in. thick by 1 in. wide by 4 in.

Flat-head screw

Adjust fence so that the workpiece is proud of the jig front.

Recess, ¼ in. x 1 in. x 5¾ in.

Workpiece

Flat-head screw, 1¼ in., is screwed directly under the center of the clamp.

Hardwood guide piece

CUTTING PROFILES. The author uses this long-grain sled when routing profiles on long, narrow boards. The toggle clamps are safer and more effective than using fingers to guide the work this close to a cutter.

between the router insert and the tabletop, these imperfections will be transferred to the workpiece. The top must also be as square to the spindle as practical.

The fence must be straight, flat, and square to the top. Adjustability would be nice, but if it ain't flat and straight, the depths of cut will vary, and there may be some risk to the user.

A Bit about Cutters

Router bits come in many diameters, lengths, and shapes. Some are easy to use, and some, in my opinion, require extra vigilance on the part of the operator. A bit must be sharp to cut cleanly. No matter how skillful you may be, you cannot get good cuts from a dead bit.

Certain cutters—because of their size and shape—require special skills and jigs to achieve good results. I think most woodworkers are unaware of this. Not surprisingly, manufacturers of router bits advertise a bit's application, not its difficulty in use. For instance, cutters that are over 2¼ in. dia. are adapted from other cutters designed specifically for the shaper spindle. Manufacturers present these cutters to the amateur as being like any other tool bit in their inventory. But they are not. The bits require special methods for controlling the workpiece, slower speeds, and advanced operator skill.

Moreover, there is no way these bits can cut their profiles in one pass; often three or four are required. A consequence of taking multiple swipes is that the bits dull pretty quickly. You can expect a good cutter to have a half-life of 200 ft. to 300 ft., if the bit is treated with respect. I wouldn't say to rule out large cutters entirely; they are going to be popular no matter what I say. Instead, I recommend using them with extreme caution: Take light cuts, practice, be sure the workpiece is secured firmly, and use special fences or guards to keep your hands away from the bit.

Horsepower vs. Human Power

It is fairly easy to push wood across a router table, so you may tend to feed stock too quickly. To compensate for this, I recommend using as large a router as possible in a table—ideally a 2½-hp to 3-hp model. A large router not only provides pure muscle but also evens out any balance problems with a bit, and the "flywheel" action keeps the cutter moving uniformly. That said, a 1½-hp router with a sharp cutter will work for short runs and light cuts (the equivalent of a ⅜-in. by ⅜-in. cut). However, if it's working more than 30 minutes or if you're

Use Spacers for Stepped Cuts

SET THE CUTTER FOR THE DESIRED DEPTH. Stack ¼-in.-thick MDF spacers underneath the workplace and remove one after each cut. A metal rod secures the spacers while the length of the cut is determined by a stop block over the fence.

SMALL BITES WITH LARGE BITS. Large cutters last longer and yield a cleaner cut when the cut is made in small stages. Four ¼-in.-thick pieces of MDF are placed against the fence and secured over a metal rod.

A SIMPLE, EFFECTIVE FENCE

You can get by with a piece of MDF or jointed hardwood as long as it is straight. A pivot point at one end makes fine adjustment easier. The other end is secured with a C-clamp.

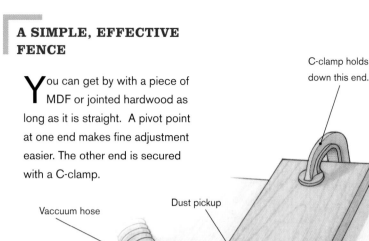

C-clamp holds down this end.

Vacuum hose

Dust pickup

Fence is typically only a few inches longer than the router table. Thickness is a minimum of ¾ in., but 1 in. is preferable.

Cutout for bit clearance

Pivot point is secured to the table.

FENCE AND CUTTER SETUP. Using a sample with the desired final profile, establish the correct height of the cutter and the final position of the fence (top). Mark this location by clamping a registration block to the table (center). Make stepped cuts by moving the fence back in stages (bottom). The final cut will be with the fence against the registration block.

making larger cuts, a small-horsepower router may tend to overheat. Routers with 1 hp or less should be confined to bits with ¼-in.-dia. shanks. A big cutter in a small router is a recipe for poor-quality cuts.

Determine the Feed Rate for Every Cut
Feed rate on the router table is not fixed and must be learned for each combination of router, workpiece, cutter design, sharpness, and depth of cut. If the feed rate is too slow, you can burn the work and destroy the cutter. If you feed the work faster than the cutter can cut and eject its chip, you may chatter the work or break the bit.

Production shops aim for maximum productivity with minimum adversity, and you should too. Even the fanciest of production shops relies on the test cut. Once you are set up, test the process. Start with a feed rate that's almost slow enough to burn the stock and increase the speed to the point of tearout. Although many factors affect the feed rate (such as the hardness of the wood and the sharpness of the bit), in general you can achieve a quality cut at a steady rate of about 20 ft. per minute. Remember, just as it takes some time getting used to a new set of golf clubs, it will take some practice to get familiar with the correct feed rate for a new setup.

Tips for Smooth Cutting

There's more to achieving good results on a router table than just the equipment and the feed rate. You need well-prepared stock, secure hold-downs when necessary and good working habits. With practice, the following guidelines will ensure consistent, satisfactory results with your table-mounted router.

Begin with Good Stock Preparation

Material preparation cannot be overlooked in any aspect of woodworking. But routing, due to its methods of registering the work to the cutter, is more sensitive to misshapen work than most tools are. A stick with a crook, cup, or bow is not to be trusted. One that is poorly jointed or not uniform in thickness will be a surprise during each operation, and the resulting cut will be a disappointment. Improperly prepared stock is also a safety issue: Warped stock cannot be cut accurately and may be hard to push past the bit, increasing the chance of injury.

Get a Grip on Your Work and Stop Chattering

Like a group of mischievous lads, a router can get where no other tool can. You can enter the edge, the end, or the face of nearly any stick. The cut can be blind, half-blind, through, or cut to any fractional depth.

A router bit can't be expected to behave without adversity under all of these conditions. A cutter can chatter the walls and floors of its pathway. It can tear out as it encounters wavy grain. It can burn in cherry and spoil the entry and exit of cross-grain cuts such as dadoes. A bit can break, bend, burn, vibrate, scream, lose its carbide, or go dull in seconds if it's abused.

To combat these problems, it is the accepted practice to use hold-downs, featherboards, and other contrivances to manage difficult cuts on the router table. I don't. In my view, if the operation is a risky one, it requires a proper jig to control the workpiece safely and achieve a quality cut.

Over the years I've developed numerous jigs for use with a router, but two simple ones will aid many of your cuts on the router table. The first is an end-grain sled (see the drawing on p. 117) used when cutting the end of a workpiece, particularly a narrow one. The work is secured with toggle clamps, and a backup piece of scrap can be placed between the workpiece and the jig's fence to prevent breakout.

The second jig is a long-grain sled (see the drawing on p. 118) used when routing the face of long, narrow stock, where control by fingertips alone would be an accident waiting to happen. Stock that is rigidly held, not resonated with a featherboard, will be chatter-free.

Think about How You're Working

The ergonomics of table routing is also important. I see many woodworkers stand in front of the table and feed the work hand over hand in a series of jerky movements. For a smooth cut you need one long, flowing movement, and this can come only if you stand at the front corner of the router table on the infeed side. Use your right hand to provide the forward momentum and the left hand to direct the workpiece down and against the fence.

Take Light Passes

If a new cutter is making a mess of the workpiece, you're probably trying to take off too much wood at once. The solution is to take lighter cuts, adjusting the depth of cut until the quality is acceptable. The starting point may cause the bit to cut far less than the profile itself, but it has to be your starting point or you'll kill the cutter or mutilate the workpiece. You can adjust the depth of cut by lowering the cutter, by shimming the workpiece or by making adjustments to the fence.

There are three ways to adjust the depth of the cut without adjusting the cutter. The first method is to use spacers under the workpiece. A second way is to use spacers against the fence. Spacers allow you to cut the profile in increments, easing the strain on the equipment and giving a cleaner cut (see the sidebar on p. 119).

The third way can be used with any type of fence (see the photos on the facing page): First establish the location of the fence during the final depth of cut using a sample with the finished profile. Clamp a registration block at this point, and then move the fence forward so that only a small part of the cutter is revealed. Make the first cut. After the first cut, gradually move back the fence, taking incremental cuts until the fence is resting against the registration block. Now you're ready for the final cut.

Strategies for Special Cuts and Bits

There are several cutting strategies that will render the cut safe and of maximum quality. For example, skinny moldings can be harvested off wide stock, broad rabbets on narrow stock can be "tunneled" first and then ripped, and large cuts can be done in two or more stages. Special strategies are also required for trapped cuts, dovetail cuts, and climb cuts.

Trapped Cut When the cutter is trapped in the work, such as when profiling a stile, it can lift the work and spoil the profile. For cuts like this, stock must be well-prepared (flat and straight) and under firm control using a long-grain sled.

Dovetails For a smooth cut, a dovetail bit usually requires its path to be preplowed with a straight bit. This strategy also prevents the bit from breaking.

Instead of gradually raising the straight-cut bit, which can be backbreaking if you don't have a router lift, you can vary the height of the workpiece via stackable spacers. Take multiple passes, removing the spacers—I use ¼-in.-thick medium-density fiberboard (MDF)—one at a time. When the workpiece is resting on the surface of the router table, you're ready to make the final cut, with the bit having to establish only the finished profile.

Climb Cutting These cuts should be made only by those with experience on the router table. The purpose of feeding the wood in the same direction as the turning cutter is to get a very smooth cut with no tearout. If the operator loses control, the workpiece is propelled off the table and can pull the operator's hands into the router bit. Take only very small cuts, and make sure that both the workpiece and the fence are perfectly straight.

When to Go with a Handheld Router

I stated earlier that the majority of cuts are best performed on the router table, but there are some cuts that are either safer or better when done with a handheld router. These include cuts on long boards, particularly the ends, profiles on the edges of large tabletops, inside cuts and cuts best made with a plunge router. To table-rout for these cuttings is to ask for trouble.

PAT WARNER is a woodworker and college instructor who lives in Escondido, California.

Bench-Mounted Router Table

I was getting ready to make grand-father clocks—one for each of my three children—and I needed a router table. The clocks entailed routing lots of curved moldings, raised panels, and long boards, and their imminence finally forced me to think about designing a router table that would suit my needs. Because of the limited floor space in my basement shop, I hesitated to build a freestanding unit. And I discarded the idea of building a table where the router would sit on my work-bench because it would make the work surface too high to work at comfortably.

It occurred to me that I could make a suitable router table that took advantage of the features of my very sturdy 8-ft.-long cabinetmaker's workbench, if I could design the table so that the router hung below the workbench surface. In effect, my router table is really only a router tabletop in that it has no legs and gets its sturdiness from being clamped to the bench. The table has three parts: the main table, which is the

BY PAUL MANNING

THIS THREE-PART TABLE clamps to a workbench and it hangs from the ceiling when not in use.

NO LEGS REQUIRED

This table gets its sturdiness from being clamped and bolted to the author's workbench. The dimensions of the table are determined by the shape and size of the bench to which it will be mounted.

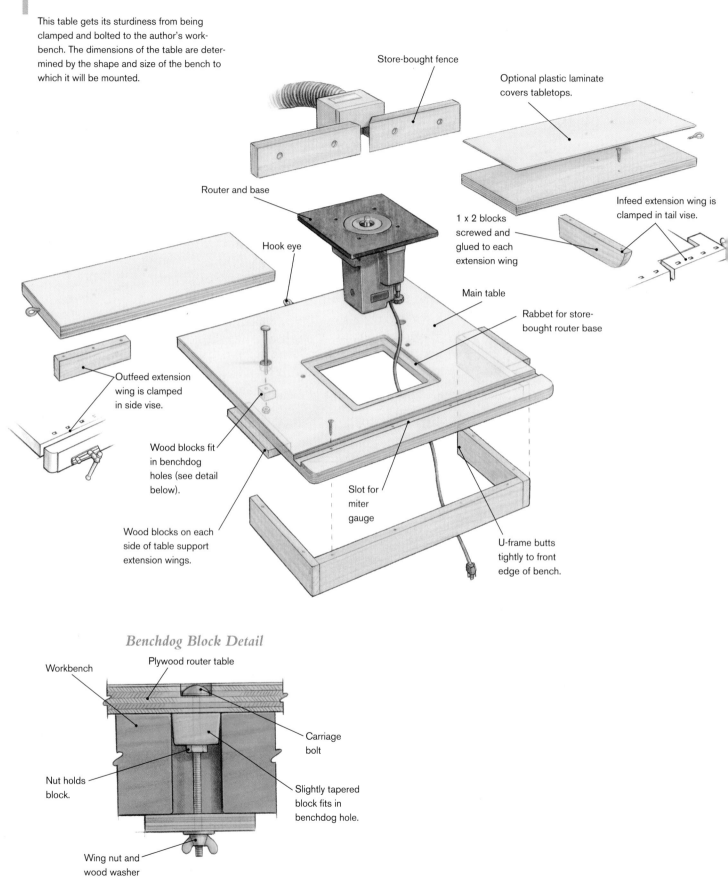

Store-bought fence

Optional plastic laminate covers tabletops.

Router and base

1 x 2 blocks screwed and glued to each extension wing

Infeed extension wing is clamped in tail vise.

Hook eye

Main table

Rabbet for store-bought router base

Outfeed extension wing is clamped in side vise.

Wood blocks fit in benchdog holes (see detail below).

Wood blocks on each side of table support extension wings.

Slot for miter gauge

U-frame butts tightly to front edge of bench.

Benchdog Block Detail

Workbench

Plywood router table

Carriage bolt

Nut holds block.

Slightly tapered block fits in benchdog hole.

Wing nut and wood washer

center section that holds the router and fence, and infeed and outfeed extension wings, which are clamped in the tails and side vises, respectively. Best yet, when I'm not using the table, the whole thing hangs on hook eyes from my basement ceiling joists, freeing up valuable floor space.

Buy the Fence and Build the Table from Scraps

I bought a phenolic-resin router-base insert and a cast-aluminum router fence from Trendlines for about $120. I had been thinking about building a fence, and while toying around with a design idea, I came across what I thought was a perfectly adequate system from Trendlines. The system has 14-in.-long adjustable fences and a dust-collection port that plugs right into my shop vacuum.

My bench is very heavy. Even with the weight of the router and the 13-in. cantilever of the router table, the bench is sturdy enough that it won't tip forward, and thus no supporting legs are needed under the front edge of the table.

My main table is 30 in. wide and 24 in. deep, but obviously you'll have to size your table to fit the size and shape of your workbench. The most important dimension is the location of the router itself. It should be mounted as close as possible to the front edge of the workbench. The extension wings can be of any length and width, but I made mine 6 in. narrower than the front edge of the main table so that I can stand close to the working router bit.

The tabletop extends beyond the U-frame, permitting the use of clamps for featherboards and hold-downs and making room for a miter-gauge slot. The extensions have short pieces of hardwood underneath for insertion into the bench vises.

Assembly Suggestions

After cutting the plywood for the main table, I transcribed the locations of two bench-dog holes onto the plywood. To register the bench-dog blocks in the holes, I glued and loosely bolted each one to the plywood with a short bolt. While the glue was still wet and the bolts were loose, I inserted the blocks into the bench-dog holes. I then tightened the bolts and quickly removed the table.

After the glue dried, I replaced the short bolts with long carriage bolts, inserted the table into the bench-dog holes, and fixed the table to the bench with wing nuts (see the drawing on the facing page). Holding the U-frame tightly against the front of the bench, I clamped it to the plywood, then screwed through the tabletop and into the U-frame.

For the extension wings, I clamped cleats in the bench vises and then aligned the tops of the extension wings, pushing them tight to the main-table edges. Then I screwed through the extension wings and into the cleats.

Note in the drawing that a block of wood is also glued and screwed under the main table's ends and protrudes 1 in. to provide a shelf support for the extension wings and to keep all surfaces in the same plane.

The table is well sealed with polyurethane, and the top surfaces are covered with plastic laminate. The plastic laminate is not an absolute necessity; a table that is well sealed and sanded smooth should be satisfactory. The grandfather clocks, by the way, turned out great.

PAUL MANNING lives in North Andover, Massachusetts.

Sources

Trendlines
888-234-8665

Horizontal Router Table

This easy-to-build table cuts tenons fast and accurately.

BY ERNIE CONOVER

Being a traditionalist, I favor using mortise-and-tenon joints in all frame construction. For years I have cut tenons on the table saw with a tenoning jig, and I still favor this method for large tenons. For ¾-in. stock, I became convinced that it would be child's play to build a simple table that would effectively cut tenons in almost all situations. This table, designed and made with the help of my friend Dave Hout, can be built in about two hours, works better than commercial tables of a similar ilk, and is small enough to be stored out of sight when not needed.

I made the table of medium-density fiberboard (MDF), but good-quality veneer-core plywood would work, too. Simple biscuit joints hold the table together. I used ¾-in. material for the bottom and sides and a double thickness for the top. The same material can be used if you wish to construct a miter gauge. The swing arm was made of ½-in. veneer-core plywood, as were the front and back ends, and the adjusting screw block can be made from any hardwood. While it is tempting to cover the table with plastic laminate, a couple coats of white shellac will give plenty of wear resistance.

Any 1½-hp router that handles ½-in. bits will work in the table. The router does not have to be super-adjustable. Because the

Simple to Build, Easy to Use

This horizontal router table is made of ¾-in.-thick MDF and ½-in.-thick plywood joined with biscuits. Almost any type of non–plunging router is suitable, and depth and height adjustments are easily made.

DEPTH ADJUSTMENT. The depth of the cut is controlled using the adjustment gauge on the router.

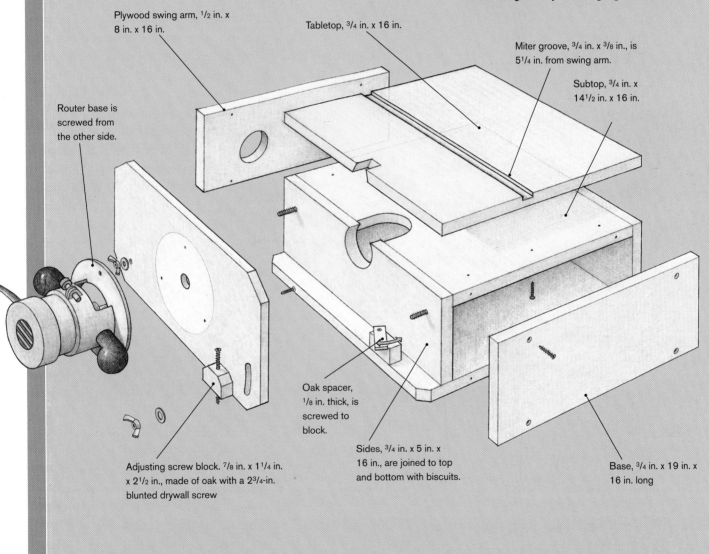

Plywood swing arm, ½ in. x 8 in. x 16 in.

Tabletop, ¾ in. x 16 in.

Miter groove, ¾ in. x ⅜ in., is 5¼ in. from swing arm.

Subtop, ¾ in. x 14½ in. x 16 in.

Router base is screwed from the other side.

Adjusting screw block. ⅞ in. x 1¼ in. x 2½ in., made of oak with a 2¾-in. blunted drywall screw

Oak spacer, ⅛ in. thick, is screwed to block.

Sides, ¾ in. x 5 in. x 16 in., are joined to top and bottom with biscuits.

Base, ¾ in. x 19 in. x 16 in. long

majority of tenons cut by my machine are ¾ in. long, the router-bit depth is seldom changed. The adjustment that controls tenon thickness is tweaked frequently, but it's done using the screw in the screw block, not the router itself. In short, when it comes to routers, an old clunker will do.

The table is easy to use. A ¼-in. tenon is correct for ¾-in. stock, yielding approximately a ¼-in. shoulder, depending on the stock thickness. In most situations, the shoulder dimension can be carried all the way around the tenon. This works splendidly because four quick cuts yield a perfect tenon. With a narrow rail (1 in. or less), a smaller shoulder at the top and bottom is desirable. In this case, you can either move out the ⅛-in. spacer below the adjusting screw to reduce the shoulders by the same amount or place a ⅛-in.-thick shim under the rail while cutting. For a haunched tenon, a spacer block of the same thickness as the groove in the adjoining post is interposed between the stock and the swing arm before starting the cut where the haunch is desired.

A backer board to help avoid tearout is seldom necessary if you use the sequence of cuts shown in the photos below. The first breakout is to the back side of the rail, and the remaining three breakouts are inconsequential. I use a ½-in. solid-carbide spiral-fluted (two flute upcut with 1¼ in. of flute) router bit. The upcut design pulls the stock against the swing arm, which is just where it should be. Resharpened bits are fine for use in this table because the exact diameter of the bit is unimportant.

By plunging the bit through the swing arm after mounting the router, you get a zero-clearance opening that prevents small tenons from dropping into a void around the cutter. Most shavings end up under the table, but to ensure this you may have to widen this opening below the surface. By closing the open ends of the box with ½-in. plywood, a shop vacuum or dust collector can be connected to the table to minimize dust. Once finished, you will find the table so useful that it will not gather dust!

ERNIE CONOVER runs Conover Workshops in Parkman, Ohio.

Accurate Results

By turning the wood in a clockwise motion away from you, the breakout is confined to the initial cut. Follow the sequence in the photos below to maintain consistent height and depth through all four cuts.

HEIGHT ADJUSTMENT. Fine-tune the height of the router bit by turning the screw in the screw block. When correct, tighten the wing nuts on the swing.

The Ultimate Router Table

BY JOHN WHITE

I have always been dissatisfied with the popular designs for router tables and the versions available on the market. In some way or another, they are all less convenient than standard woodworking machines. For one thing, you have to reach under the table a lot to adjust bit height, change bits, or hit the power switch. The ultimate router table would be as convenient as a shaper or table saw—all of the common tasks and adjustments are done from above or outside the unit. It would also have the dust-collecting ability and vibration-dampening mass of a cabinet-mounted tool.

I came up with a router cabinet that meets all of the above criteria and is super-quiet to boot. The design relies on the JessEm Rout-R-Lift, a screw-driven mechanism that allows you to raise and lower the router and bit by cranking a handle inserted from above. The JessEm unit is also sold by Jet as the Xacta Lift, for the same price—around $200 in many catalogs. By adding a shopmade mounting block to the lift, I was able to raise the router high enough to allow bit changes from above the table as well.

Eliminating the need to reach underneath the top let me mount the table on a cabinet, which could enclose a shop vacuum and muffle its sound and the roar of the

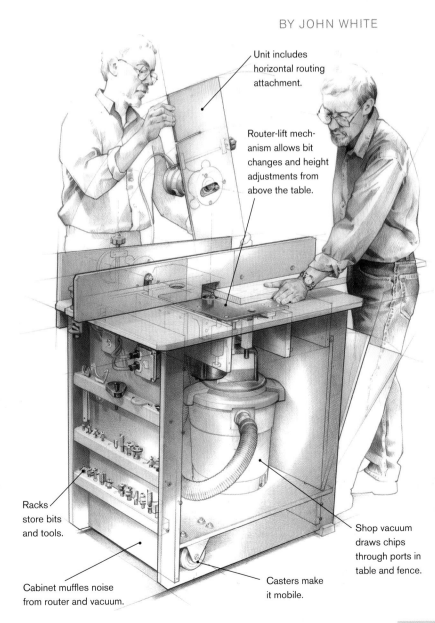

Unit includes horizontal routing attachment.

Router-lift mechanism allows bit changes and height adjustments from above the table.

Racks store bits and tools.

Cabinet muffles noise from router and vacuum.

Casters make it mobile.

Shop vacuum draws chips through ports in table and fence.

Simple Parts, Smart Function

The cabinet is made entirely from ¾-in.-thick MDF joined with knockdown fasteners. The front-to-back braces below the tabletop support the router plate and double as the sides of the dust manifold. Two filler blocks close the gap around the lift mechanism, which makes for efficient dust collection.

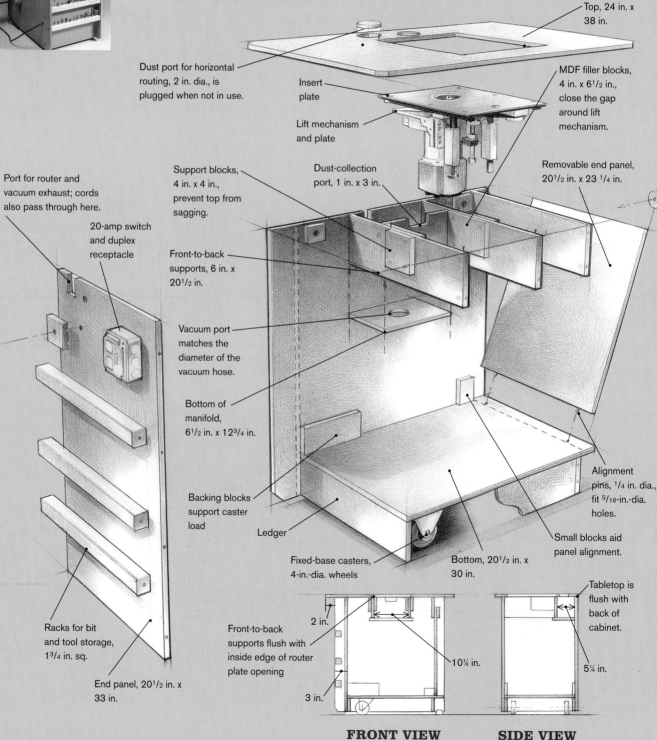

Top, 24 in. x 38 in.

Dust port for horizontal routing, 2 in. dia., is plugged when not in use.

Insert plate

MDF filler blocks, 4 in. x 6½ in., close the gap around lift mechanism.

Lift mechanism and plate

Removable end panel, 20½ in. x 23¼ in.

Port for router and vacuum exhaust; cords also pass through here.

Support blocks, 4 in. x 4 in., prevent top from sagging.

Dust-collection port, 1 in. x 3 in.

20-amp switch and duplex receptacle

Front-to-back supports, 6 in. x 20½ in.

Vacuum port matches the diameter of the vacuum hose.

Bottom of manifold, 6½ in. x 12¾ in.

Alignment pins, ¼ in. dia., fit 5/16-in.-dia. holes.

Backing blocks support caster load

Ledger

Small blocks aid panel alignment.

Fixed-base casters, 4-in.-dia. wheels

Bottom, 20½ in. x 30 in.

Racks for bit and tool storage, 1¾ in. sq.

End panel, 20½ in. x 33 in.

Front-to-back supports flush with inside edge of router plate opening

Tabletop is flush with back of cabinet.

2 in.

10¼ in.

5¼ in.

3 in.

FRONT VIEW   **SIDE VIEW**

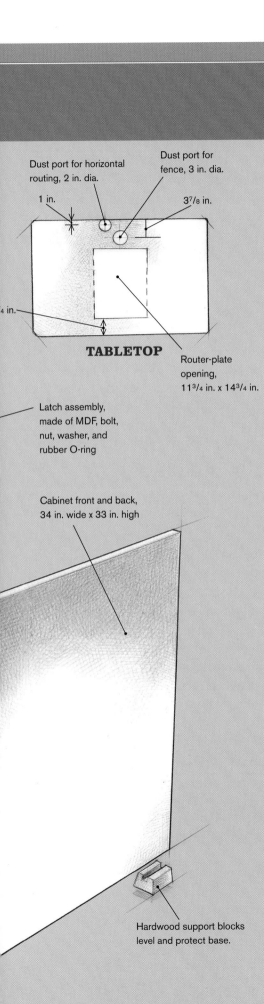

Dust port for horizontal routing, 2 in. dia.

Dust port for fence, 3 in. dia.

1 in.

3⁷/₈ in.

⁴ in.

TABLETOP

Router-plate opening, 11³/₄ in. x 14³/₄ in.

Latch assembly, made of MDF, bolt, nut, washer, and rubber O-ring

Cabinet front and back, 34 in. wide x 33 in. high

Hardwood support blocks level and protect base.

router itself. A dust-collection manifold fits under the tabletop and behind the lift unit. A fence system with a dust port ties into the system below.

I mounted a switched outlet for the router and vacuum unit outside the cabinet. Just for fun, I threw in racks for bit and tool storage. Casters under one end of the cabinet make it mobile—like a wheelbarrow— but still stable on the floor.

Materials cost just over $300, including the shop vacuum and the router lift but not a fixed-base router (the more powerful, the better for use in a table). The investment in time and money was significant but reasonable, considering the performance and convenience I gained.

MDF and Knockdown Fasteners

The entire unit—cabinet, table, and fence—is made of ¾-in.-thick medium-density fiberboard (MDF), with two coats of Watco oil for added durability. I used MDF because it offers flatness, mass, and stability at a very low cost. To make sure the cabinet would remain sturdy, I opted for cross-dowel knockdown fasteners over glue and screws. Casters and wood blocks keep the MDF edges off the floor, where they might soak up moisture and then fracture.

Cutting out the MDF parts should be straightforward, but be sure to wear a dust mask, and don't count on the factory edges of the panels being square. Squareness and accuracy are very important with such a large cabinet, especially with interior parts that must fit tightly. Chamfer the edges of the tabletop to prevent chipping. This isn't a bad idea for the other MDF parts, as well. I used a laminate trimmer with a 45° router bit to zip quickly along the many edges.

I have a few tricks for drilling accurate holes for knockdown fasteners (see the sidebar on p. 132). On the back side and tabletop, counterbore the heads of the fasteners to maintain a flat surface.

Knockdown Fasteners Make Strong Joints

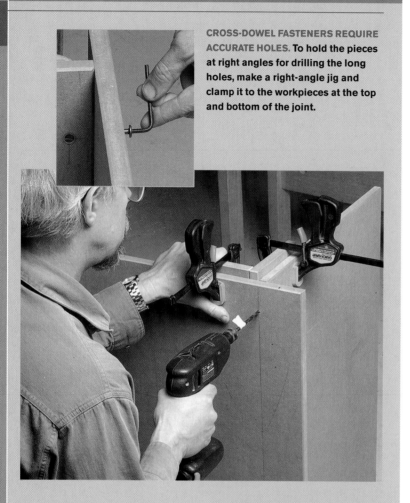

CROSS-DOWEL FASTENERS REQUIRE ACCURATE HOLES. **To hold the pieces at right angles for drilling the long holes, make a right-angle jig and clamp it to the workpieces at the top and bottom of the joint.**

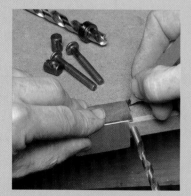

ALUMINUM FLASHING MAKES A LAY-OUT JIG FOR THE CROSS-DOWEL HOLES. **With a drill bit in the bolt hole, use the jig to locate the center-point of the cross-dowel hole.**

THE CROSS DOWELS WILL BE INVISI-BLE IF YOU DON'T BREAK THROUGH THE OUTSIDE. **Use a stop collar to control the depth.**

To support the casters, install backing blocks inside the cabinet. Assembled, this unit weighs more than 100 lb.

Installing the Access Panel One end panel is removable so that you can open the cabinet and empty the shop vacuum. Size this panel to fit the cabinet walls snugly, but overlap the support strip at the top of the opening. Drill two ¼-in.-dia. holes in the bottom edge of the panel for the pins or cutoff bolts that will keep the panel in position. Press the pins into the panel, then drill ⁵⁄₁₆-in.-dia. holes in the base of the cabinet to receive the pins. Glue the two stop blocks to the walls of the cabinet, which will make it easier to put the panel quickly back in position.

Add the latch assembly. I recommend placing a rubber O-ring under the rear washer to regulate the action of the latch.

Router Lift Requires an Exact Cutout

The only tricky procedure on the tabletop is making a precise cutout to fit the router-lift insert plate. Start by flipping over the top. Lay out the front edge of the cutout 3 in. from the front edge of the tabletop. Then lay the lift-plate assembly on the tabletop, locating its front edge along the layout line. Next, screw MDF strips around the edges of the insert plate, being careful not to punch through on the top side. In addition, to avoid too snug a fit (MDF swells in high humidity), add a layer of masking tape along the edges of the guide strips before attaching them to the underside. These strips will guide your jigsaw and router cuts.

Keep the jigsaw cut about ¼ in. away from the strips; the router will handle the rest. Then remove the masking tape, and rout the finished opening. A ¾-in.-dia. pattern-cutting bit will leave the correct ⅜-in. radius at the corners to match the lift plate.

Router Lift Is the Heart of the Table

It all started with the JessEm Rout-R-Lift™, which allowed White to design a cabinet-based unit that encloses dust-collection and muffles noise yet puts all controls and adjustments on the outside.

LEVELING SCREWS OFFER PRECISE ADJUSTMENT. The weight of the router lift is carried by the two front-to-back braces, instead of the tabletop as is the case with most router tables.

A CUSTOM ROUTER MOUNT FOR EASY BIT CHANGES

Replacing the router's base with a shop-made mounting bracket allows the nose of the router to be raised high enough for wrenches to reach it.

NO REACHING BELOW TO ADJUST HEIGHT. The adjustment crank is inserted from above.

Drilling Vacuum-Port Holes There are a number of large holes in this unit. I use an adjustable-wing circle cutter (or fly cutter) for all of these. (For a video clip on using this tool, go to finewoodworking.com.) A wing cutter must be used in a drill press. Proceed slowly and with caution, keeping your hands and clothing well clear of this whirling dervish of a bit.

The large hole in the tabletop connects the fence's dust port with the dust-collection system below. Another one is necessary if you opt for the horizontal router attachment. In that case, one of these holes should always be

Make an Accurate Cutout for the Insert Plate

MDF GUIDE STRIPS ENSURE ACCURACY. Lay the insert plate on the underside of the tabletop and screw on the strips. A layer of tape leaves room for seasonal movement of the MDF.

THE STRIPS GUIDE THE JIGSAW. Make the rough cutout about ¼ in. from the MDF strips.

THEN THEY GUIDE THE ROUTER BIT. Remove the tape, and use a bearing-guided bit to cut the opening flush with the strips. A ¾-in.-dia. bit will leave a ⅜-in. radius at the corners.

plugged when the other is in use. Attach fender washers on the underside of the table around each hole to support the plugs.

Support Structure Aids Dust Collection

With the top completed, you are ready to assemble the support structure below. The two main braces for the router-lift insert plate also serve as the sides of the dust-collection manifold at the back of the cabinet. Locate and attach these pieces first.

Secure these front-to-back braces so that their outside faces are just even with the edges of the insert-plate cutout. Then attach the notched crosspiece, positioning it to miss the lift mechanism by 1/16 in. or less. The smaller the gap here, the less suction lost around the lift plate. The notch in the crosspiece is a dust port that draws air through the bit opening into what will be the dust manifold. Now cut out the piece for the bottom of the manifold and use the wing cutter to drill a hole for the vacuum hose. Only a cutoff section of the vacuum hose will fit into the cabinet, so size the hole in the box for the hose diameter, not an end coupling. Lock the hose in place

with two fender washers positioned to catch the spiral grooves in the hose. Screw the bottom piece to the manifold.

A few steps remain to create good air suction through the bit opening. Attach another layer of ¾-in.-thick MDF to each support brace, along its inner face, to create a close fit around the sides of the insert plate. Then, using double-sided tape and/or screws, attach a thin metal flap (I made mine from aluminum flashing, about 0.020 in. thick) to the insert plate, as shown in the drawing on the facing page, to deflect the exhaust blast from the router motor and to allow air and chips to be drawn into the dust manifold.

Last, screw two blocks to the outside of the large front-to-back braces to prevent the tabletop from sagging near the opening in the middle of the plate.

Mount the Router in a Shopmade Base

Fine-threaded drywall screws in the support braces act as levelers for the four corners of the insert plate. MDF loves to split at its edges, so drill pilot holes for any screws, making them slightly larger than usual. I typically go with drywall screws that are at least 2 in. long. Normally, coarse-threaded screws are better for MDF, but these levelers are for fine adjustment.

You'll have to mount the router body in a shopmade base to position it high enough in the table to allow bit changes to be made from above. (The router's original base can be mounted and left on the horizontal routing attachment on the back of the table.) But you can skip this step if you don't mind removing the router-lift mechanism from the table to change bits.

Use a wing cutter to drill a large hole, exactly the size of your router body, through a block made of two thicknesses of MDF. Then cut a thin kerf through the edge of the block to allow for tightening, and drill the long hole for the tightening bolt. Attach the mounting block to the lift plate with coarse-threaded drywall screws.

Install Switch Box and Fence

I mounted a 20-amp switch and outlet box on the end of the cabinet to connect the vacuum and router to one easily accessible on/off switch. I also mounted a small block next to the box to act as a cord manager.

The fence is joined with long drywall screws but incorporates a dust box that ties into the dust-collection manifold through a hole in the tabletop. Also, a sliding face allows the fence to have an interchangeable center insert. Carriage bolts and wing nuts lock the sliding face in position.

Pipe clamps make a simple clamping system, gripping the edges of the table but also sliding freely. Drill small holes through the adjustable jaws of the pipe clamps, and screw them permanently into place.

Creating this "ultimate router table" takes some time and money, but the added precision and ease of use will reward you many times over.

JOHN WHITE is a contributing editor and the shop manager for *Fine Woodworking*.

Follow the Airflow

The vacuum draws air and chips through the bit openings in the table and fence, into the dust manifold and down the hose into the vacuum, where the dust and chips are filtered out. An angled flap of sheet metal deflects the router's exhaust blast away from the bit opening and into the cabinet.

ANOTHER IMPORTANT MODIFICATION TO THE ROUTER LIFT. A square of aluminum flashing–bent slightly and attached with double-stick tape or screws–deflects the router's exhaust into the cabinet, allowing chips to be sucked past the bit.

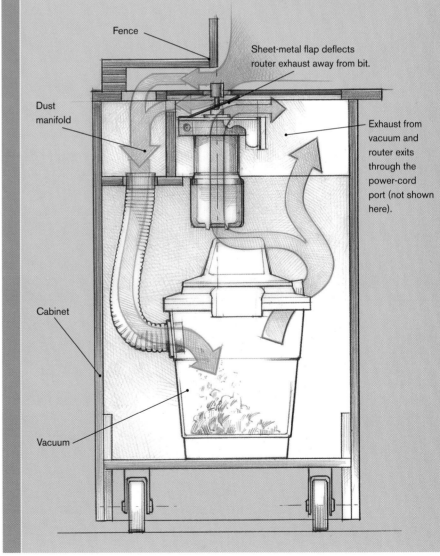

Fence

Sheet-metal flap deflects router exhaust away from bit.

Dust manifold

Exhaust from vacuum and router exits through the power-cord port (not shown here).

Cabinet

Vacuum

Simple but Effective Fence

The fence features a removable insert, a dust manifold that ties into the one below the table, and modified pipe clamps that grab the table edges.

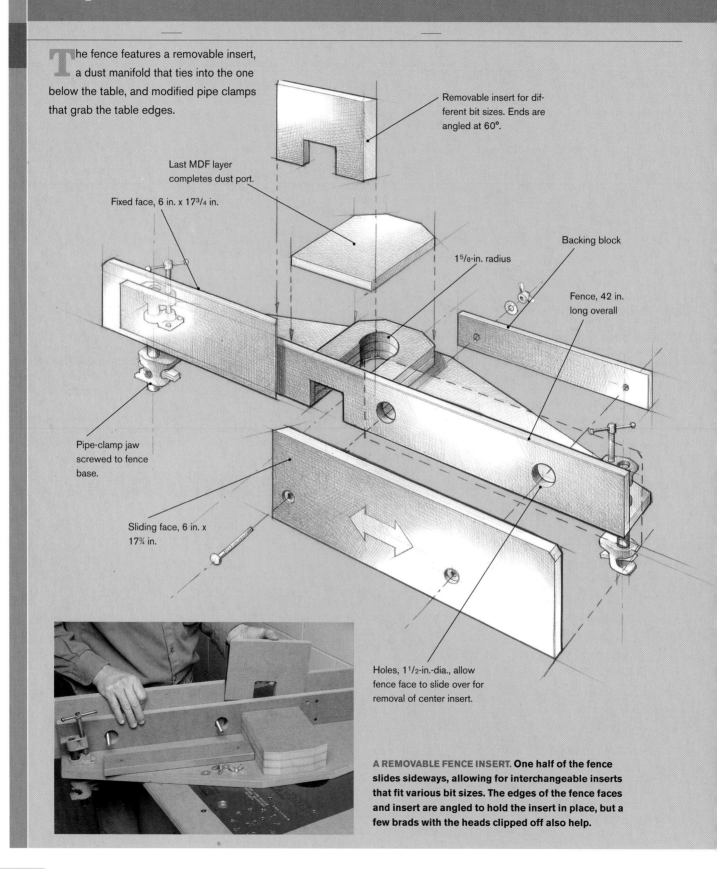

Removable insert for different bit sizes. Ends are angled at 60°.

Last MDF layer completes dust port.

Fixed face, 6 in. x 17³⁄₄ in.

Backing block

1⁵⁄₈-in. radius

Fence, 42 in. long overall

Pipe-clamp jaw screwed to fence base.

Sliding face, 6 in. x 17¾ in.

Holes, 1¹⁄₂-in.-dia., allow fence face to slide over for removal of center insert.

A REMOVABLE FENCE INSERT. One half of the fence slides sideways, allowing for interchangeable inserts that fit various bit sizes. The edges of the fence faces and insert are angled to hold the insert in place, but a few brads with the heads clipped off also help.

Horizontal Routing Attachment

The back of the table is flush with the cabinet so that the author could include a horizontal routing attachment—useful for making tenons, raised panels, and sliding dovetails, among other operations.

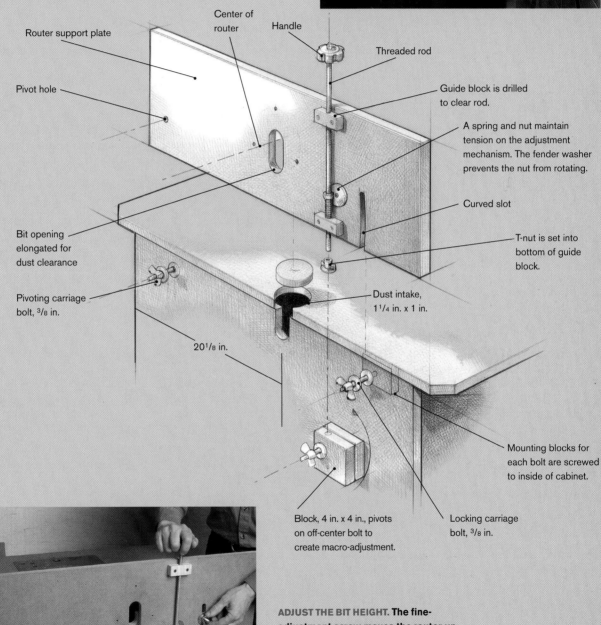

Router support plate

Center of router

Handle

Threaded rod

Pivot hole

Guide block is drilled to clear rod.

A spring and nut maintain tension on the adjustment mechanism. The fender washer prevents the nut from rotating.

Curved slot

Bit opening elongated for dust clearance

T-nut is set into bottom of guide block.

Pivoting carriage bolt, 3/8 in.

Dust intake, 1 1/4 in. x 1 in.

20 1/8 in.

Mounting blocks for each bolt are screwed to inside of cabinet.

Block, 4 in. x 4 in., pivots on off-center bolt to create macro-adjustment.

Locking carriage bolt, 3/8 in.

ADJUST THE BIT HEIGHT. The fine-adjustment screw moves the router up and down, and the clamping bolt locks everything in place. A coil spring keeps tension on the screw, preventing it from drifting as a result of vibration.

Template Routing Basics

BY PAT WARNER

In 24 years of self-taught woodworking, I've made a lot of mistakes. Early in my career, I discovered what looked like a devilishly simple technique for cutting dadoes. I used a board clamped across the workpiece to guide the router base. The first dado looked great, but the second wandered visibly off course.

The best way to guide routers is by using templates. The router registers against a template, using it as a guide through the cut. The simplicity of templates, though, gives no hint of how powerful a tool they make the router.

The router's usefulness and versatility begin with the tremendous variety of bits that are available. With only a ball bearing on the end of the bit as a guide, you are really limited to detailing edges. When you use a template, however, you free the router from following the edge of the workpiece. The router becomes capable of two more fundamental woodworking tasks: milling repeatable patterns and all kinds of joinery.

You can easily make your own inexpensive, simple, and accurate templates for a wide variety of joints and patterns. The initial investment of time to make a template for a precise task is well worth it. Your router will perform that task far faster and far more reliably than other tools can.

Templates will allow you to repeat cuts and shapes perfectly, but only if you remember to use the same bit with the same collar at the same depth. The best place to record this information is directly on the template itself.

Make Precise Templates

The best way to learn the basics of template routing is to make and use some simple templates. But before looking at the practical applications for templates illustrated on these pages, it's a good idea to start with some general advice about how to make them, what materials to use, and the best ways to use them.

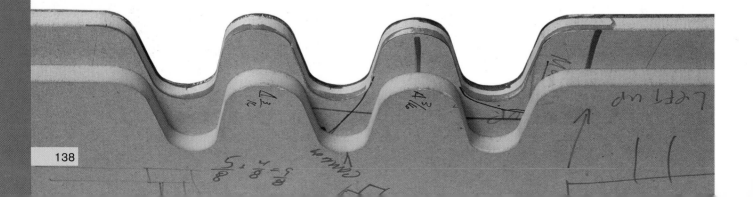

The most difficult part of template routing is making the template itself. All the important information about the final shape you want to rout is encoded in the design of the template. The more accurately you make your templates, the more time you'll save in the long run. You'll do less sanding, fitting, and fudging afterward.

Sawing, rasping, and filing are time-consuming and tedious ways to make templates. It's also very hard to make a perfect curve with hand tools. I never make a template by hand unless there is no other way. I've found that accurate templates are most easily made with sanders and, yes, routers, templates, and other guides.

Templates should be dimensionally stable, durable, and capable of taking fine details. Solid wood is a poor choice because it's not dimensionally stable. Steel is stable and durable, but to a fault. If you accidentally touch a spinning bit to it, you'll probably wreck both the bit and the template. Acrylic and Lexan are transparent and allow you to see the work beneath. They also won't kill bits. But be aware that a slow bearing will generate enough heat from friction to melt them. Medium-density fiberboard (MDF) is the best all around choice. Mind you, it isn't perfect. It's toxic and unpleasant to work with.

Four Everyday Templates

You can use any one of the three kinds of router bits designed for template work. Each has its own strengths and weaknesses (for more, see the sidebar at right). Some bits are especially well suited to certain kinds of templates, but all of them can bring speed and reliability to repetitive work.

Template for Repeatable Shapes Using a scroll saw and an oscillating sander to make a single curved shape, like a decorative shelf support, might be just as fast as template routing it. But only the first time.

Three Bits for Routing with Templates

Straight Bits and Collar Guides Are the Most Versatile

Collars are not as accurate as bearings, but they have the decided advantage of allowing you to cut at any depth in both side and bottom cuts. Fitted to the router's base and used with straight bits, they work much like pattern bits. Collar guides also act as a shield for the bit. You'll find that you will inflict a lot less injury to the template and the work by using them.

Collar guides do have disadvantages. Because the collar must be larger in diameter than the cutter, the line of cut is displaced from the template. This offset means the finished work will never be exactly the same shape as the template. And collar guides are never exactly concentric with the bit: $1/16$ in. eccentricity is typical. A way to compensate for this is to keep the same part of the collar in contact with the template throughout the cut.

Pattern Bits Are the Most Accurate

I choose pattern bits when I need the most accuracy. The bearings are typically concentric to the bit within .002 in. or better. Bearings do not leave as smooth a cut as collar guides, though the difference is generally minute. This is due to the way bearings can bounce against the template ever so slightly and very rapidly.

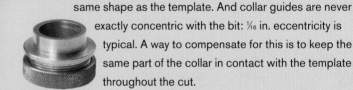

Over time, this bouncing tends to wear the template edge unevenly.

The biggest disadvantage to bearing bits is that they're restricted to a small range of depth settings. The bearing must always engage the edge of the template. I've also found that bits of this design often have diameters slightly larger than their bearings. If you run this kind of bit with some of the cutter in contact with the template, you'll rout away some of the template. Measure your bits with calipers or test them to make sure this doesn't happen.

Flush-Trimming Bits Are the Most Common

The main advantage to using flush-trimming bits for template work is that they are easier to find and slightly cheaper than pattern bits. They also come in smaller diameters than pattern bits, allowing cuts into tighter inside curves.

Otherwise, they have many disadvantages. Bottom cuts such as mortises are impossible. In other applications, the workpiece can hide the template from view, and the router must ride on the work. If it's a small or thin piece, the router will not be stable.

Cutting Multiples

A straight bit and collar guide make a good combination for cutting a stack of profiled pieces, like decorative shelf supports. The bits can cut stock of any thickness and will produce a smoother edge than a bearing-guided bit. One thing to keep in mind: The template and the finished piece will not be identical because the collar guide keeps the bit away from the edge of the template.

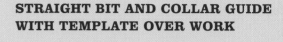

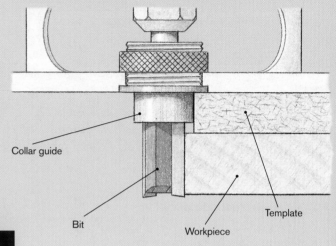

Collar guide

Bit

Workpiece

Template

If you make any more, template routing will be faster and easier. A router bit leaves a much smoother edge than a scrollsaw, and the edge will need far less sanding. Make the template much the way you would make the support if you had no templates. Smooth, gradual curves on MDF are best obtained by sanding to layout lines on a stationary belt sander.

For this kind of work, it's easiest to use a straight bit with a collar guide because you can adjust the cutting depth to match the thickness of the shelf-support stock (see the sidebar on p. 139). Collar guides, however, will displace the cut from the exact edge of the template. With straight lines, this merely entails positioning the template the offset distance from the layout line. The lines will be just as straight.

It's a different story with curves. A collar will make the bit cut slightly larger radii on outside curves and smaller radii on inside curves. The result will be a finished piece slightly different from the template. In complementary template work, this is a

Template for Butt Hinge Mortises

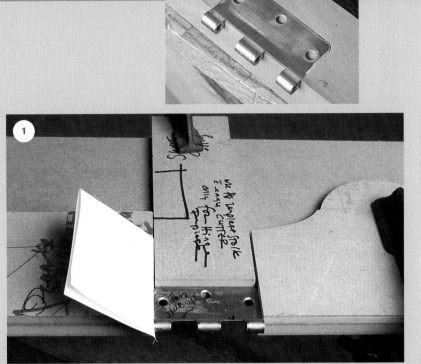

A pattern bit is a good choice for cutting shallow mortises precisely and quickly. To make the template, align the hinge on a piece of template stock, and then mark the outline with a pencil. Bandsaw out most of the waste, and reposition the hinge on the template stock. Clamp straight-edged scrap around the hinge to define the edges of the mortise (1). A paper shim will prevent the mortise from being too tight. Then remove the hinge, and rout to the line with the scrap as a guide (2). Remove the scrap, and you have a finished template that cuts an accurate mortise (3).

MAKING THE TEMPLATE

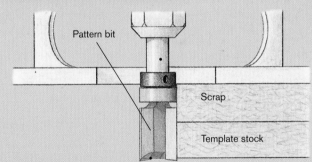

Pattern bit

Scrap

Template stock

CUTTING THE MORTISE

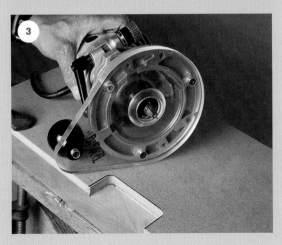

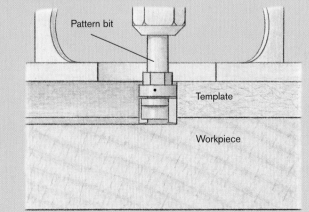

Pattern bit

Template

Workpiece

Template for Routing Small Pieces

Templates can be made so they hold small pieces as well as guide the router. Coupled with a pattern bit, this template makes short work of cutting tapered coffee table legs. The workpiece is held on the template with toggle clamps. To keep toggle clamps out of the way while routing, the author flips the template upside down on the workbench. Blocks between the template and the bench provide room for the toggle clamps.

USE A PATTERN BIT FOR TAPERED LEGS

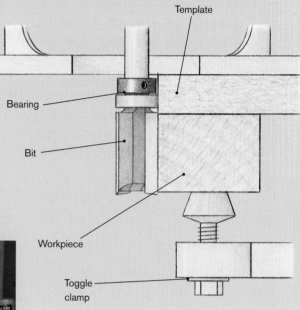

Template

Bearing

Bit

Workpiece

Toggle clamp

crucial consideration. But with something like the profile of a shelf support, the difference is inconsequential. To tell where the bit will actually cut, run a pen in a loose bearing with the same offset as the collar along the template to draw the layout line.

Cutting Shallow Mortises Cutting shallow mortises that are clean and evenly deep—like those that you would want for butt hinges—is a difficult task with traditional tools. Except for the very smallest hinges, a router guided by a template will give you more accurate cuts faster and with less variation between them. The photos and drawings in the sidebar on p. 141 show you how to make one.

Once you've made this template well, it's hard to go wrong using it as long as you are careful. Router stability on the template is essential to an accurate and safe cut. A 6-in. round base router with a ½-in.-dia. bit will have no more than 45% of its footprint on the template in an edge cut. If you make a turn around a 90° corner, that percentage is reduced to less than 20%. A router that wobbles with a lot of cutter engaged can break the cutter, tear the stock and template, or even cause a kickback that sends the router to the floor. The machine has to stay flat and stable at all times.

This butt hinge has rounded corners the same diameter as the bit. If it had square corners, you'd have to do some handwork to make the hinge fit. A bit with a larger diameter than the corners would also require handwork. Just never use a bit with a smaller diameter, or you'll have gaps to patch.

Cutting Tapers on Small Pieces Some workpieces are far too small to rout safely if they are sandwiched between a workbench and a template. To taper legs for a coffee table, for instance, I built a template (or a jig, if you like) that holds the workpiece firmly in place with toggle clamps, as shown on the facing page. Guide blocks position the side and end of the leg but leave enough room behind them to clamp the template upside down to a workbench edge. In use, neither the toggle clamps nor the clamps holding the template to the bench get in the way.

To get a good, smooth taper, you need only secure the guide blocks at the desired angle in relation to the edge of the template. As the router follows the edge, it cuts the taper angle of the blocks in the leg. Compared with table saw techniques that require more complex jigs, put fingers at risk, and leave a coarse cut, this one is far superior.

Template for Through Mortises The plunge router is the best tool for inside template cuts, such as mortises, but it needs a lot of support to make it safe and accurate. Plunge routers are top heavy and have comparatively small bases. This makes them excellent candidates for router teeter-totter problems. A template for mortising must be

large enough so that the plunge router's base is completely supported by the template at all times during the cut. The sidebar above shows a very simple technique to make a through mortise deeper than any bit you own.

PAT WARNER is a woodworker and college instructor who lives in Escondido, California.

Routing a Through Mortise

Deep mortises can be cut accurately by starting with a template and straight bit with a collar and finishing up with a flush-trimming bit. First rout the mortise as deeply as you can with the template as a guide (1). Then drill through to the other side. Remove as much waste as you can, and then flip the workpiece over (2). A flush-trimming bit that follows the upper part of the previously cut mortise will finish the job.

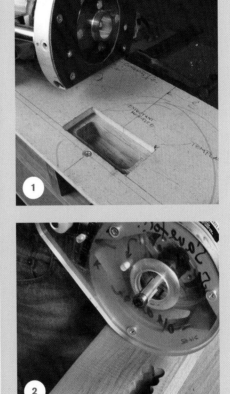

FIRST PASS WITH PATTERN BIT

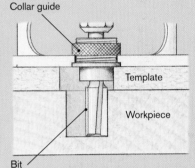

Collar guide
Template
Workpiece
Bit

FINISH WITH FLUSH-TRIMMING BIT

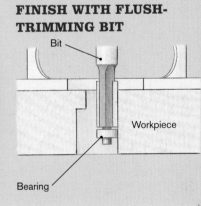

Bit
Workpiece
Bearing

Router Template Collars

BY PAT WARNER

It's true that a router can sometimes be used freehand. But because it has a dangerously sharp bit spinning rapidly at the end of a powerful motor, a router is more safely used with accessories that help the operator gain control: router tables, edge guides, add-on bases, shopmade and commercial jigs, bits with shaft-mounted bearings, and template collar guides. Each brings its own advantages in specific routing situations. But none of these router accessories adds more safety, indestructibility, ease of setup, and usefulness at an absolutely cheap cost than template collar guides. I can't imagine being without them.

A good set of seven collars often costs no more than $30. Yet, these little metal bushings that clip or screw into the subbase of virtually any router can simplify most cross-grain cuts—including sliding dovetails, mortises, tenons, dadoes, butt-hinge recesses, and stair risers—and can be used for lettering, inlaying, and even jointing short stock. The only other piece of equipment you really need in most cases is a scrap of medium-density fiberboard (MDF) or plywood used as a template to guide the collar, and thus the bit, through the cut. Collars come in different inner and outer diameters to accommodate a variety of bits and templates.

Collars Are Very Easy to Use

A collar screws or locks into the opening on the subbase of a router and extends below the subbase to ride against a template or jig. With the template clamped to the work or the work clamped to a jig, the collar rides along the template edge. The cut of the bit then mimics the template edge, whether straight or curved.

Router novices often make these cuts with the large router subbase riding against a jointed board or template. But router subbases are notoriously out of round, or non-concentric. A collar guarantees a much truer cut. For example, many of the dovetail jigs on the market use collar guides to ensure uniform and tight-fitting dovetails.

One suggestion for using a collar: There is little reason that it needs to extend more

COLLARS HAVE THE EDGE. A collar and a perfectly straight, simple template can help a straight or spiral bit put a finished edge on long grain or end grain.

than ⁵⁄₁₆ in. below the router subbase, because most templates are less than ½ in. thick. The extension should always be shorter than the template. Collars often come in ⅜-in. or ¾-in. lengths, so shorten them with a hacksaw to make them more functional.

Why Not Just Buy Bearing-Guided Bits?

Bearings are perfectly round, so for exacting work, a bearing-guided bit might be better than a collar. However, the collar is cheaper and more versatile. The collar shields the template, and the operator to some extent,

from an accidental cut. I can't tell you how many times I have ruined a template with a bearing-guided bit. A bearing-guided bit also doesn't let you plunge cut, because the bearing must remain against a template throughout the cut. And one of the biggest advantages of a collar-guided bit is that the bit can be exposed below the router at exactly the required cutting depth, whereas a bearing-guided bit must be fully extended to engage its template.

One of the biggest, yet rarely mentioned benefits of collar template guides over bearing-guided bits is that collars help

What's Your Collar Size

Router collars come in a variety of fastening arrangements, including locknut, snap-in, and screw-in types.

THE INDUSTRY STANDARD. The Porter-Cable screw-in locknut system, which works in all 1¾₁₆-in. subbase openings, is used by many other router companies.

A COUPLE OF SCREWS. Some routers with larger subbase openings, such as Makita® and Hitachi, offer a system of collars held in by two screws. Each is unique to the brand.

QUICK-CHANGE, SNAP-ON COLLARS. To avoid screws and locknuts, Bosch's guide system relies on snap-in collars that require only a twist to lock them in place.

TWO-WAY SYSTEM. Milwauke router collars are inserted from the inside of the subbase and secured with screws. They also accept Porter-Cable collars.

preserve the lives of the bit and the router motor. When using a collar, any excessive side load is transferred to the collar and subbase rather than to the bit and router, as they would be with a bearing-guided bit.

Collars are available for virtually all routers, whether fixed base, plunge, trim, or table. The most popular system is also the oldest: the two-component nut and collar ring originally produced by Porter-Cable. The Porter-Cable collars fit routers with a 1³⁄₁₆-in. hole in the subbase, including most Porter-Cable, DeWalt, Black & Decker®, Skil®, Elu, and many Hitachi models. Other router companies sell either adapters or their own collar systems—or both (see the sidebar on the facing page).

Grooves and Dadoes

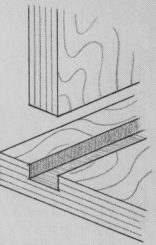

A STRAIGHT PATHWAY. There is probably no better way to cut cross-grain dadoes than using a collar. Dadoes deeper than ⅛ in. can be cut in a series of passes. Grooves that run with the grain are cut the same way.

Mortise and Tenons

YOU NEED A JIG FOR TENONS. With a shopmade jig that will clamp the work vertically, a collar can be used to cut cheeks and shoulders of tenons at the same time.

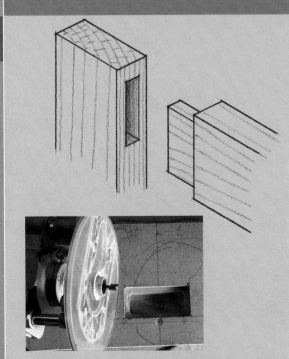

LESSEN THE RIGORS OF CUTTING A MORTISE. A simple template clamped to a workpiece or a door will make cutting mortises easy with a collar.

Sliding Dovetails

SLIDING DOVETAILS ARE A
BREEZE. Using a collar and template is a slick way to cut the slot for a sliding dovetail. The same setup can be used to cut out some of the waste with a smaller straight bit before cutting the dovetail.

Limitations Are Minor

There are a few limitations to using a collar, but they can be easily overcome. Using a collar often means that less than half of the router subbase is supported during the cut. This is especially dangerous with plunge routers, which tend to have small subbases and tip more easily. There are a couple of things you can do about this. I think bigger offset subbases are such a good, safe idea for all routers that I manufacture them on the side. An offset subbase keeps the router flat, stable, and under control. With a plunge router, try to use a template that completely surrounds and

supports the subbase whenever possible (see the sidebar on the facing page).

A second, minor problem with a collar is that the bit is rarely exactly in its center, even though the collar is round. So it is important to keep the same edge of the collar against the template throughout the cut, ensuring a straight result. To help guide the router, draw a line on your template with a marker. Keep the same part of the router subbase, or the handle of the subbase, on that line. For situations in which you need absolute concentricity, use the more expensive, shaft-mounted, bearing-guided bit. But a collar, especially when

Subbases for Added Stability

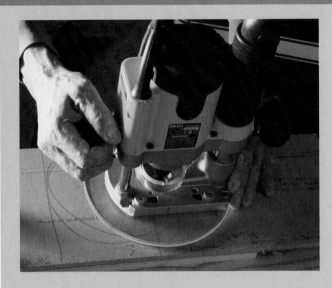

PLUNGE ROUTERS REQUIRE SPECIAL ATTENTION. When routing with a collar on a top-heavy plunge router, it is best to attach a larger subbase for safety and stability. Whenever possible, use a template that supports the router on all sides.

AN OFFSET SUBBASE IS A GOOD IDEA. An offset subbase will help steady a router with a collar attached. You can correct for any lack of concentricity in the collar by keeping the same edge of the collar against the template. Do this by drawing a line on the template and guiding the subbase handle along that line.

used with an offset subbase, will be accurate enough for most woodworking cuts.

Other Limitations Be careful to set the depth stop on a plunge router so that the spinning collet nut does not hit the inside of the collar. Also, with the popular, two-piece Porter-Cable collar system, the collar can unscrew itself if you move the router around the template in a clockwise direction (an ill-advised climb cut). A little twist with channel-locking pliers before routing will prevent it.

Most collars have a maximum 1⅛-in. inner diameter, so they will accept cutters up to only about 1 in. dia. For general and straight-edge cutting, this matters little, but for some decorative template routing with form cutters, bearing-guided router bits may be required because they are available in cutter sizes larger than 1 in. dia.

Despite these negligible restrictions, when you add it all up, collar template guides really pay their way. They're cheap, safe, versatile, and never wear out—a rather rare collection of benefits for such an ordinary accessory.

PAT WARNER is a woodworker and college instructor who lives in Escondido, California.

Credits

The articles in this book appeared in the following issues of *Fine Woodworking*:

p. 4: Routing Safe and Sound by Pat Warner, issue 129. Photos on p. 4 by Scott Phillips, courtesy *Fine Woodworking*, © The Taunton Press, Inc.; Photos on pp. 5–7 by Strother Purdy, courtesy *Fine Woodworking*, © The Taunton Press, Inc.; Drawings © Vince Babak

p. 8: Routers for Router Tables by Patrick Warner, issue 141. Photos by Anatole Burkin courtesy *Fine Woodworking*, © The Taunton Press, Inc. except photo on p. 11 (bottom right) and p. 13 (bottom) © Patrick Warner.

p. 14: Tune Up Your Router by John White, issue 152. Photos by Tom Bengal, courtesy *Fine Woodworking*, © The Taunton Press, Inc.

p. 21: All about Router Bits by Jeff Greef, issue 116. Photos on pp. 21, 24–26 by Scott Phillips, courtesy *Fine Woodworking*, © The Taunton Press, Inc.; Photos on pp. 22–23, 26–28 © Jeff Greef; Drawings © Bob La Pointe, courtesy *Fine Woodworking*, © The Taunton Press, Inc.

p. 30: Spiral Router Bits vs. Straight Router Bits by Pat Warner, issue 140. Photos on pp. 30–32 by Michael Pekovich, courtesy *Fine Woodworking*, © The Taunton Press, Inc.; photos on pp. 33 (top photos)

and 34 (top) by Tim Schreiner, courtesy *Fine Woodworking*, © The Taunton Press, Inc.; Photo on p. 34 (bottom left) © Dennis Preston; Antique Scale on p. 31, courtesy of E.Buk, Spring Street, NYC.

p. 35: Router Bits Tackle Cope and Stick by Jeff Greef, issue 107. Photos by Sloan Howard, courtesy *Fine Woodworking*, © The Taunton Press, Inc. except photo on p. 35 © Jeff Greef; Drawing © Heather Lambert.

p. 42: Spline Joinery by Steven Cook, issue 109. Photos by Vincent Laurence, courtesy *Fine Woodworking*, © The Taunton Press, Inc.

p. 46: Mortising with a Router by Gary Rogowski, issue 121. Photos by Vincent Laurence, courtesy *Fine Woodworking*, © The Taunton Press, Inc.; Drawings © Jim Richey.

p. 55: Floating-Tenon Joinery by Lon Schleining, issue 158. Photos by Asa Christiana, courtesy *Fine Woodworking*, © The Taunton Press, Inc.; Drawings © Vince Babak.

p. 61: Router Fixture Takes on Angled Tenons by Edward Koizumi, issue 114. Photos by Vincent Laurence, courtesy *Fine Woodworking*, © The Taunton Press, Inc. except p. 62 © Boyd Hagen, courtesy *Fine Woodworking*, © The Taunton Press, Inc.; Drawings © Heather Lambert.

p. 68: End-Work Router Fixture by Patrick Warner, issue 96. Photos © Patrick Warner; Drawings © Vince Babak.

p. 72: Turn a Router into a Joint-Making Machine by Guy Perez, issue 103. Photos by Alec Waters, courtesy *Fine Woodworking*, © The Taunton Press, Inc.; Drawings © David Dann.

p. 80: Make Your Own Dovetail Jig by William H. Page, issue 106. Photos by Charley Robinson, courtesy *Fine Woodworking*, © The Taunton Press, Inc.; Drawings © Vince Babak, courtesy *Fine Woodworking*, © The Taunton Press, Inc.

p. 84: Shopmade Dovetail Template by James Buxton, issue 143. Photos by Anatole Burkin, courtesy *Fine Woodworking*, © The Taunton Press, Inc.; Drawings © Vince Babak.

p. 89: Compact Tool Makes Dadoes a Snap by Skip Lauderbaugh, issue 110. Photos by Alec Waters, except p. 92 photo by Kent Ezzell, courtesy *Fine Woodworking*, © The Taunton Press, Inc.; Drawings © David Dann courtesy *Fine Woodworking*, © The Taunton Press, Inc.

p. 94: Micro-Adjustable Tenon Jig by Pat Warner, issue 135. Photos by Dennis Preston, courtesy *Fine Woodworking*, © The Taunton Press, Inc.; Drawings © Melanie Powell.

p. 99: Shop-Built Horizontal Mortiser by John F. Matousek, issue 142. Photos by Jefferson Kolle, courtesy *Fine Woodworking*, © The Taunton Press, Inc., except p. 100 photos by Michael Pekovich, courtesy *Fine Woodworking*, © The Taunton Press, Inc.; Drawings © Bob La Pointe.

p. 103: Micro-Adjustable Router Fence by Pat Warner, issue 144. Photos by Michael Pekovich, courtesy *Fine Woodworking*, © The Taunton Press, Inc.; Drawings © Peter Goncalves @ Design Core.

p. 110: No-Frills Router Table by Gary Rogowski, issue 123. Photos by Vincent Laurence, courtesy *Fine Woodworking*, © The Taunton Press, Inc.

p. 115 Get the Most from Your Router Table by Pat Warner, issue 157. Photos by Mark Schofield, courtesy *Fine Woodworking*, © The Taunton Press, Inc.; Drawings © Vince Babak, courtesy *Fine Woodworking*, © The Taunton Press, Inc., except drawing on p. 116 by Erika Marks, courtesy *Fine Woodworking*, © The Taunton Press, Inc.

p. 123: Bench-Mounted Router Table by Paul Manning, issue 134. Photos by Jefferson Kolle, courtesy *Fine Woodworking*, © The Taunton Press, Inc.; Drawings © Bob La Pointe.

p. 126: Horizontal Router Table by Ernie Conover, issue 147. Photos by Mark Schofield, courtesy *Fine Woodworking*, © The Taunton Press, Inc.; Drawings © Vince Babak, courtesy *Fine Woodworking*, © The Taunton Press, Inc.

p. 129: The Ultimate Router Table by John White, issue 153. Photos by Asa Christiana courtesy *Fine Woodworking*, © The Taunton Press, Inc.; Drawings © Bruce Morser.

p. 138: Template Routing Basics by Pat Warner, issue 125. Photos by Strother Purdy, courtesy *Fine Woodworking*, © The Taunton Press, Inc.; Drawings © Vince Babak.

p. 144: Router Template Collars by Pat Warner, issue 139. Photos by Tim Schreiner, Drawings © Vince Babak.

Index